D1826539

UNMASKING THE SPIRIT OF INJUSTICE

The Truth Never Before Revealed
Behind Our Daily Struggles

ANGELA STRONG

WESTBOW
PRESS®
A DIVISION OF THOMAS NELSON
& ZONDERVAN

Scripture quotations are taken from The Holy Bible, New International Version®, NIV® Copyright © 1973, 1978, 1984, 2011 by Biblica, Inc.® Used by permission. All rights reserved worldwide.

WestBow Press books may be ordered through booksellers or by contacting:

WestBow Press
A Division of Thomas Nelson & Zondervan
1663 Liberty Drive
Bloomington, IN 47403
www.westbowpress.com
1 (866) 928-1240

Because of the dynamic nature of the Internet, any web addresses or links contained in this book may have changed since publication and may no longer be valid. The views expressed in this work are solely those of the author and do not necessarily reflect the views of the publisher, and the publisher hereby disclaims any responsibility for them.

Any people depicted in stock imagery provided by Getty Images are models, and such images are being used for illustrative purposes only. Certain stock imagery © Getty Images.

ISBN: 978-1-9736-5691-3 (sc)
ISBN: 978-1-9736-5693-7 (hc)
ISBN: 978-1-9736-5692-0 (e)

Library of Congress Control Number: 2019902915

Print information available on the last page.

WestBow Press rev. date: 03/21/2019

PREFACE

I am very pleased that you have chosen this material to read! My desire is that these revelations of the Holy Spirit may be a blessing for your life, and the entire body of Christ.

I feel a great sense of relief to have exposed the operations (or the means of attack) of this often subtle spirit from the kingdom of darkness, which is constantly working behind the scenes of all the terrible acts of injustice that occur in our lives and in our nations.

Through this book, you not only discover the existence of this evil spirit, but you will also be empowered with the necessary spiritual strategies to win your spiritual battles. You will be guided step by step in how to fight against this evil spirit, and how to be free from his attacks. Through this book, I will show you how to bind the influence of this malignant spirit over your life and family, how to stop its cruel operations over your nation and how to cancel its attacks over your ministry.

The revealed truths in this book will show you the reasons behind the cycles of tragedy and injustice that have been occurring in your life and why you constantly feel that you are swimming against the current. If It seems that you can't advance in your life no matter how hard you try, or you feel like there is some kind of force blocking or detaining you from reaching the next level, this book is for you.

This journey is also designed to bring inner healing to your life, and free you from all emotional wounds that this horrible spirit might have left in your life due to its acts of injustice.

It is my greatest desire that you, the reader, are completely delivered from all bindings and oppressions caused by this malignant spirit, and that you are empowered to free others as well.

It is my purpose that you be able to walk in the freedom, good health, abundance, prosperity and fulfillment that God has designed for you.

It is my greatest motivation to wake up the Body of Christ, the Church, about the clandestine operations of this evil force, thus allowing all believers to occupy their watchful position in God's kingdom, as well as to become the voice of his wonderful and liberating message. All this revelatory information will open your spiritual eyes, to position you into the special place of governorship that our Heavenly Father has destined for you.

PROLOGUE

At the end of each year, like most people do, I make a list of all my New Year's resolutions about all the things that I wish to accomplish for the next year.

I found myself making this list at the end of 2009, with one exception. I had reduced my long list of goals to just one: to build a much closer and more intimate relationship with the Holy Spirit.

This singular goal ended up changing my whole life! Even though I was born into a Christian home, I was taught that the Holy Spirit was simply the third person of the Trinity.

Until my discovery in 2009, I always thought that the "third Person" meant that there existed a position of hierarchy, and that the Holy Spirit occupied that third rank. I interpreted this as the Holy Spirit being third in power, third in his influence and third in importance in God's kingdom.

This erroneous concept I had of the Holy Spirit led me to question, as many others do, why I should try and seek a relationship with the third Person, when I could go directly to the first Person.

For all my previous spiritual life, my objective was to seek a relationship with God the Father and God the Son, but I was completely oblivious to any need of the participation or presence of the Holy Spirit in my life.

In my search, I discovered that it is impossible to develop an intimate relationship with God the Father, without first establishing a relationship with the Holy Spirit. The Scriptures tell us that it is the Holy Spirit that reveals the Father to us.

It is this amazing revelation that allowed me to see a whole new perspective of my own faith. This is why I am foregoing the traditional literary rules of book writing, and instead of finding a renown author to write a forward for this book, I am writing a forward to the Holy Spirit.

It is the Holy Spirit who is the true hero of this story, so it is the Holy Spirit that deserves all the merits and accolades for the content in this book. I am merely one of his collaborators.

This is why I take the opportunity to honor the Holy Spirit for becoming my best friend, my mentor, my counselor, my provider, the one who renews my strength every day, the one who reveals all hidden mysteries of the universe and the one who guides me to all truth and justice. I would also like to honor his presence in my life, his special care, his wisdom, and his revelations; for giving me direction and for being my shield and defender.

Above all, I would like to honor the Holy Spirit for dwelling in me, and making me his temple, despite him being so holy and pure. I am certain that each truth that is revealed in this book by the Holy Spirit will break a link of the chain that has been detaining you from your destiny.

I know that the breakthrough that you have been waiting on for years will come to pass in your life. I declare that the truths revealed in this book will make you truly free, that your long wait will be over, and that as you submerge your spirit in these revelations, the Holy Spirit will bring you confirmation, and you will begin entering into the level of authority, fullness and governorship that the Father has designed for your life.

DEDICATION

I would like to dedicate this book to all the people dealing with oppositions and struggles throughout their walk toward their divine destiny. I also dedicate this book to all those believers in general that feel like they are constantly fighting against an unknown enemy.

This book is also dedicated to anyone who has fallen victim to unjust circumstances. This includes people who have had the misfortune of being born in countries that are filled with corruption, discrimination, abuses of power, human rights violations, and where human trafficking and all kinds of injustices occur on a daily basis.

I dedicate this book to those who have stumbled over and over again, who have been on the very brink of giving up, but instead clung to the promises that God has made to them.

I dedicate this book to those who have been waiting for divine justice to be manifested in their favor. To those who have found refuge in the words of the Master when he says, "Blessed are those who are thirst and hunger for justice, for they shall be quenched" (Matt. 5:6).

I dedicate this book to two amazing women of God: Christine Caine and Joyce Meyer, for their inspiring fight against human trafficking and sexual slavery.

I also want to dedicate this book to those who, despite all the hardships they have gone through along the road to their destiny, still feel a sense of hope in their spirit, and still believe that it hasn't all been for nothing. For those who wish wholeheartedly to be led by the Holy Spirit in how to operate in a greater dimension of spiritual warfare.

This book is also dedicated to those who are tired of living under the same cycles of oppression which have kept them stagnant for years. For those who want to actually produce a radical change in their lives, in their ministry or in their nation. For all those who would like to bring back the designs and principles of the kingdom of God to their circumstances.

I also dedicate this book to all believers who are waiting for the physical manifestation of God's promises in their lives.

Finally, I would like to dedicate this book to my husband Ross, who was personally attacked in many areas of his life by this evil spirit, and for whom this book has shed so much light on the numerous questions he's had during his walk with Christ.

INTRODUCTION

I used to be intrigued by the question of why bad things happen to good people. Why is it that the innocent have to suffer? Why does it seem as though evil appears to always override the good?

What is even more surprising to me is to see some people, families, ministries, and nations be recurring victims of constant tribulations without any apparent provocations or viable reasons.

To see how faithful believers in God and his Word fall victim to constant cycles of injustice, including repeat patterns of early death in the family, repeat patterns of tragic accidents, constant cycles of divorce, cycles of sexual abuse, cycles of human exploitation, and cycles of family violence.

To see hard working, active people die before they get to see the fruits of their labor. By the same token, to see people that work hard all their lives and never seem to prosper. It seems as though all these people are constantly swimming against the current, struggling to prosper or even just get by. To see them wonder if they are fighting against some sort of invisible force that is constantly against them, preventing them from reaching their goals, or even receiving a just compensation for their hard work.

To see innocent children become victims of physical and sexual abuse, or even child labor exploitations. Little girls that are sold, sometimes by their own parents, to be prostituted.

To see women that fall victim to false promises, and later are forced into prostitution through intimidation or trickery.

All these circumstances bring us to ask ourselves the million dollar question, "Why do so many acts of injustice occur in a world that is governed by a good, almighty and all-powerful God?"

This also forces us to consider why acts of injustice keep multiplying on a daily basis. Why, after so many years, are we still fighting against slavery, human trafficking, and the exploitation of minors and yet, have not been able to abolish them?

According to the United Nations, more than 40 million people around the world were victims of modern slavery, forced labor and forced marriage in 2016 alone. This was noted to be more slaves than at any other time in human history.[1]

Further, according to the U.S. State Department, there are between 600,000 to 800,000 people being trafficked annually, of which 80 percent are women and 50 percent are minors.[2]

What is the driving force behind all these practices? Why do they maintain themselves so boldly? Why do these evil activities keep growing each year, despite the human efforts that are made to combat them?

Why is it that the just must pay for the bad actions of others? Why have evil acts taken the front stage of popularity in our nation, as well as in the lives of some believers?

What is the spiritual force behind all these acts of injustice and suffering which cause so much emotional pain to its victims and their loved ones? Why have all these bad things created such uncertainty and unrest around this planet and all its people?

Actually, the spiritual force behind all these human catastrophes has a complete name and it is called "the spirit of injustice." This is the well-hidden truth behind all the struggles and oppositions that we face on a daily basis.

This evil spirit operates in the lives of people by causing recurring and unjust events including job loss, difficulties in becoming prosperous, and false accusations. It can also operate in whole nations through tyrannical dictatorships, unjust political practices, division between social classes, abuse of power and more.

Often, this evil spirit operates within given family members, causing cycles of inexplicable tragedies such as tragic deaths, where many family members die before their time in a shocking and dreadful way. The ripples of this spirit in a family can also include a cycle of abuse or rape, or a cycle of family members becoming widows or widowers. This evil spirit can also operate in a family through cycles of divorce, as well as cycles of poverty, where no matter how hard they try to prosper, they can't see any financial progress.

This spirit of injustice also works to destroy ministries by causing ministerial stagnancy. No matter how diligently everyone is working, there seems to be no advancement in the ministry itself, disallowing financial growth, and causing inner turmoil and descent through false accusations, betrayals, criticisms, judgmental acts and more. This is all done by this evil spirit in an attempt to discredit the ministry and impede its expansion.

The main reason that the operation of this spirit has been so difficult to detect is because of the subtleness with which it makes its attacks. We remain completely unaware that we have been attacked by this sneaky spirit, until it has gained so much advantage over us that we can only see the results of its evil operations.

Even after we experience the catastrophes, the emotional wounds and the family tragedies that this slimy spirit has left in its wake, we often simply continue our suffering, and then keep asking ourselves, "Why me? Why do all these bad things happen to me? What have I done to deserve this? Will this go on forever? Why is life so unfair to me?"

When this happens, we often begin to blame God with statements like, "Why does God allow these things to happen to me? If God loves me so much, why did he allow this in my life?"

Sometimes we blame ourselves and we think that there is actually something wrong with us. We even come to convince ourselves that we actually deserve all these negative and unfair things that are happening to us.

We can also begin looking for others to blame, thus creating and harboring hatred and resentment in our hearts. All this emotional pain and confusion causes us to completely overlook the actual author of these evil events. Therefore, we begin using human solutions to fight against our situations, without obtaining any significant results.

The reason we don't see any results in our fight is because we are fighting against an actual evil spirit, under a great disadvantage of not knowing about its existence, or its slimy way of operating.

This is why I thank God for the gift of the Holy Spirit! It is the Holy Spirit that reveals this evil spirit to us and instructs us on how to overcome it, so that it cannot continue exercising authority over our lives.

In this book, I will expose the evil works of this sneaky spirit, as well as how it may attack us, how it infiltrates our lives, our families, our ministry, or even our nation. I will instruct you in how to counterattack this evil spirit, and how to cancel its operations in all areas of your life.

I will also instruct you in how to break the cycles of injustice in your own life forever, how to come out victorious from its attacks and how you can activate God's blessings over your life and household.

I have also included a declaration of renouncement against the spirit of injustice. This declaration is a prophetic declaration of deliverance from this evil spirit. In addition, I've also developed a three day journey of prayer and fasting that has been designed to guide you step by step to free yourself forever from this destructive spirit.

I also cover the topics of how to heal oneself of all the emotional wounds that this spirit of injustice causes, how to regain your self-esteem and how to retake ownership of your true identity in Christ!

I have also included a prophetic declaration of identity, which is designed to re-establish and reaffirm your true identity in Christ, as a born-again Christian. By proclaiming this prophetic declaration, you will see yourself as Jesus sees you and not the way your surrounding circumstances dictate you.

It is my objective to unmask this malignant spirit that has been attacking God's people for so many centuries, and to expose its clandestine work and practices. I want to empower the Body of Christ with the necessary spiritual weapons so that we can stand up against this spirit as the warriors God has designed us to be, and undo all evil works of the kingdom of darkness.

It is my greatest desire that you be able to reach the highest level of fulfillment that our Father in heaven intended for you before you were born, and that you may live in the freedom that God has called you to.

CHAPTER 1

One of the reasons God the Father sent his Son, Jesus Christ, down to this earth was to bring justice to all the people suffering under the immense social abuses of the Roman Empire, which were being exerted over all conquered nations.

During the time Jesus was on this earth, the social classes were controlled by the "elites." These people had control and power over all the economy, over all religions, and over all of society. This elite class was in charge of oppressing, subjugating, and enslaving the rest of the population who were not officially recognized by them as being a part of their exclusive group.

One had to be born into or obtain a certain amount of material riches and have a certain degree of formal academic studies in order to be a member of this group, which constituted about only seven percent of the total population.

Ever since the beginning of the Christian faith, there has been the divine purpose to establish a just society, free from all social inequalities, including slavery. A good example of this purpose is the story of God liberating his people of Israel from slavery in Egypt. We see this purpose rising up again when the people of Israel were enslaved by the brutal regime of the Roman Empire. We now know that God sent another liberator, who was none other than his own Son, Jesus Christ.

We now know that God sent his Son not only to die for our sins, but also to serve as a role model so that humanity could see how things really worked in God's kingdom. Jesus also came to show us how not to live according to this world filled with injustice and abuses.

Let us for a moment dabble in the historical context of Jesus. We know that Jesus was born in the province of Galilee, which was disintegrating rapidly due to the death of the Roman emperor, Herod the Great.

It is documented that Jesus lived his entire life under the cruel dictatorship of the emperor's son, Antipas. Antipas was one of Herod the Great's three sons, and was one of the cruelest rulers of his time. It is thought that Antipas inherited much of his horrific character from his father.

Antipas was the one who eliminated John the Baptist because of the criticisms John had made against the emperor while he was in the desert. In other words, Jesus was well aware of the many abuses propagated by the ruling elites of his time.

We also know that most of the working class were limited to plowing the land, spreading the seeds, harvesting their produce, and fishing in the Galilean Sea with their nets.

Unfortunately, all these working people were controlled by Antipas and his tax collectors, who were backed up by his enforcing henchmen.

Not only did the farmers have to pay huge taxes on the harvested produce, but they also had to give half of their harvest to the landlords as rental fees for the use of the land, which they could never own anyway. This was unjust and made it extremely hard for anyone to make any meaningful advancements in their lives, or the lives of their families.

It was in this horrific, unjust, and abusive atmosphere that Jesus lived, and he was well aware of its existence. In fact, Jesus even used these terrible circumstances as an example in one of his parables (Mark 12:1–9).

If we look at the historical background of the social structures that existed during the time of Jesus and analyze them in detail, we can observe that a key characteristic between the working farmers and the elites was the enormous economic disparity between them. This clearly was done to keep empowering the small group of elites at the expense of the larger, humble community of farmers.

So what ruled over all political, social, and religious systems was much abuse, intimidation, and injustice. This was done in a way so that if anyone disagreed, or even rebelled against the establishment, they would be punished immediately or would have to surrender to the life of cruelty and injustice. Jesus was sent as the sacrificial lamb to undo these evil works.

> Dear children, do not let anyone lead you astray. He who does what it right is righteous, just as he is righteous. He who does what is sinful is of the devil, because the devil has been sinning from the beginning. The reason the Son of God appeared was to destroy the devil's works. (1 John 3:7–8 NIV)

It's clear to us that Jesus was well aware of what could happen to people who confronted the unjust system of the Roman Empire. He knew it firsthand because of what had happened to John the Baptist. But none of these worldly circumstances were able to distract Jesus from focusing on the main reason he was sent to the earth: to save all souls from the slavery of sin.

Jesus was focused on changing all these social injustices and establishing human respect by loving your neighbor and introducing the concept of social equality. All these efforts ended up killing him.

The liberating message of Jesus was in fact, a very real threat to the existence of the Roman Empire that was operating under this slimy spirit of injustice. Jesus said in one of his public sermons that to enter his kingdom one must be as a child (Matt. 18:3). This was a direct challenge to the ecclesiastical establishment. You see, children were at the bottom of the social ladder and were worth nothing to the elites.

By the same token, when Jesus spoke of the equal value of a woman when he compared a woman's sin of adultery to be the same as a man's sin, this also was a huge blow to the spirit of injustice that was operating in the Roman Empire. Again, it was okay to be a polygamist if you were a man, but as a woman, it was a sin punishable by stoning to death if you were caught being an adulteress (John 8:7).

Another great example of the way Jesus crushed the spirit of injustice was the story of the woman with the issue of blood (Luke 8:43–48). Jesus even recognized when the woman had touched his garment and said that virtue had been released out of him. It was part of the law that a woman with her menstrual cycle was considered unclean and could not be out in public. Even worse, she could not touch a man who was a prophet. The woman was considered so unclean that anything she touched became unclean as well.

This was yet another clear message that Jesus sent out from his ministry—that he was vehemently against the injustices that were being waged upon women. He became the voice that advocated for equality between men and women, placing women on the same level of importance as men.

Another gigantic advance that Jesus made against the spirit of injustice was that he picked fishermen to be his disciples. Being a fisherman in those days was considered one of the lowest levels of employment, reserved for brutes and illiterates.

In Mark 12:41–44, Jesus used the example of the woman who only gave two coins as her offering, and said that she had given more than anyone else. It was considered a great offense in those days to even mention the fact that a woman gave an offering, let alone mention that she had given more than the

Sadducees (priests). Even worse than that, the comparison of a woman's offering to those of men in power was indeed a reckless disregard for the social standards. Actually, offerings were measured more by quantity than by circumstances or intentions of the heart.

The whole intention of the elites was to fight against the ideas of human equality, equal power, equal economic accessibility and equal social status. They didn't want the masses to have access to any of it. In other words, the elites wanted them to be crushed—and to be expendable.

What Jesus offered to the common person was a different outlook, a completely new perspective of how the kingdom of God really operates, even in things related to their religious customs. Jesus was representing a new form of government whereby genuine human value was given to all those forgotten and hardworking people of society.

> Jesus said, "My kingdom is not of this world. If it were, my servants would fight to prevent my arrest by the Jews. But now my kingdom is from another place." (John 18:36 NIV)

Jesus was clear in his message. His main focus was to establish God's kingdom and his justice, knowing that all other things would be added to it.

> But seek first the Kingdom of God and his righteousness, and all these things will be given to you as well. (Matt. 6:33 NIV)

One of Jesus's best examples of battling the spirit of injustice was that he was birthed by a simple town woman and had a father who was a carpenter. Both of his parents were part of this insignificant class of people who were not part of the elite.

Jesus was also born in an insignificant town called Nazareth. This small town had only about 400 inhabitants, and it was located in the lower mountains of Galilee. This poor area had their people living in caves or in very rustic shacks made out of trees.

We all know that Jesus as the Son of God, could well have chosen much better circumstances to come into this world. He could have chosen more affluent or influential parents, or maybe even chosen a more important city like the holy city of Tiberius, or even Jerusalem. Instead, Jesus chose the humble town of Nazareth.

However, we now know that Jesus intended to break with all these pre-established concepts of power in the hands of the few. He came to counterattack the notion of superiority because of political influence or because of economic status, or even because of self-proclaimed social status. Jesus came to change all this with his simple message of love, respect and true equality for everyone.

Jesus came to change the mentality of a people imprisoned by this spirit of injustice, which allowed massive fortunes to be made by the forceful oppression of the needy, where no one could access this social class, unless they were already born into it, or somehow possess the necessary educational or financial status that would allow them to be part of this selected small group.

Jesus came to remove the bandages that were covering the eyes of his people, the bandages that kept them from seeing above the unjust reality that surrounded them. Jesus came to open the eyes of all those who were being told that there was no hope for a more just and joyful life unless they showed their loyalty to the Roman Empire.

> The thief comes only to steal and kill and destroy;
> I have come that they may have life, and have to
> the full. (John 10:10 NIV)

It is for this reason that Jesus referred to his message as "the good news." Before Jesus, this phrase was allowed to be used only to announce the achievements of Caesar. However, Jesus used this phrase intentionally, to make it very clear that his gospel and everything related to the kingdom of God was the true good news.

Jesus wanted to make sure that everyone could associate the good news to the renovating message of a new kingdom, which had arrived to undo the evil works of the kingdom of darkness.

Even when Jesus was ascending into heaven, his mission to bring the government of his Father down to this earth and to keep fighting against the spirit of injustice, continued to be an essential part of his assignment.

> This is why Jesus said before he departed this earth, "I will not leave you as orphans; I will come to you." (John 14:18 NIV)

> But the Counselor, the Holy Spirit, whom the Father will send in my name, will teach you all things and will remind you of everything I have said to you. (John 14:26 NIV)

In other words, the fight against the spirit of injustice did not end when Jesus ascended into Heaven, but continues with the help of the Holy Spirit who will guide us to all truth and justice. As we know, justice is the essence of God'skingdom and it is what he rules the universe with.

> Like your name, O God, your praise reaches to the ends of the earth; your right hand is filled with righteousness. (Psalms 48:10 NIV)

So, everything that is unjust, no matter what form it manifests in, doesn't belong to the kingdom of light, but to the kingdom of darkness.

> Righteousness and justice are the foundation of
> your throne; love and faithfulness go before you.
> (Psalms 89:14 NIV)

What needs to be understood here is that when we commit unjust acts or behaviors, consciously or unconsciously, we are associating ourselves with the kingdom of darkness and we become collaborators of its evil works.

This is why God's will is that we live in the Spirit, so we may operate in sync with his kingdom and be guided by the Holy Spirit to all truth and justice.

> So I say, walk by the Spirit, and you will not
> gratify the desires of the flesh. (Gal. 5:16 NIV)

> But if you are led by the Spirit, you are not under
> the law. (Gal. 5:18 NIV)

Chapter 2

In order that Satan might not outwit us. For we are not unaware of his schemes. (2 Cor. 2:11 NIV)

As I have mentioned before, the spirit of injustice has an extraordinarily subtle way of operating and is very hard to detect when we are under its attacks or influence. This is why we need the help of the Holy Spirit, so he can lead us to the truth.

This clandestine spirit often operates through our social rules or cultures. In other words, it may seem as though we are doing a normal or common thing, when in fact, we are being manipulated by this slimy spirit.

For example, world societies are generally structured and organized in a hierarchical fashion. You have the upper class, middle class and then the lower class. These social levels not only determine the power you have to acquire things, butoften how important or influential your self-value is.

In other words, if you belong to the upper class, your life, your family and your health is often considered worth much more than if you were a member of the middle or lower class. This is also independent of whether or not you are a good and worthy human being.

In most of our world societies, a person is no longer valued for their moral or human values, but rather by their net worth. Without realizing it, many believers have been brought up with these same measures and evaluations, and begin to function in this atmosphere without actually being conscious of the fact that they are being influenced by the spirit of injustice.

So, consciously or unconsciously, we begin to treat people based on our human or cultural parameters of value and not based on their real value according to the Word of God and the divine regulations that rule his kingdom.

Another way the spirit of injustice can operate is through acts of oppression and exploitation. Just as in the Roman Empire, the spirit of injustice is alive and well when we observe the world participating in the oppression and exploitation of certain groups of people.

In most of the developing nations around the world, we can observe the many practices of exploitation with employees. Usually, these laborers are people with little education, few financial resources and limited working skills, making it virtually impossible for them to find another job.

The employer will usually pay less than the going wage for that particular job, the employees are made to work longer hours than lawfully allowed. they are also treated as inferiors, and their human rights are often violated.

So we sometimes find ourselves complicit in these unjust practices only because we have been raised in these social schemes ourselves, and it seems so very normal. We begin to rationalize it just because everyone else is doing the same thing.

Unfortunately, we don't realize that we have been sucked into the slimy grips of the spirit of injustice and we become immune to its evil ways. Without even being aware of it, we gradually become participants of this evil web, and before we know it, the spirit of injustice starts to spread into other areas of our of circumstances.

Once this starts happening, the spirit of injustice begins gaining strength and it starts expanding its tentacles into other social spheres, including the sexual exploitations of minors.

Minors are forced to do sexual favors in return for money, and the money then goes to the one exploiting the underaged child.

This spirit of injustice also operates heavily in the area of human trafficking. In most cases, women are lured from their country of origin under false promises, and then forced into prostitution.

Another way the spirit of injustice operates is through the genealogy of families. In other words, families who have received lucrative financial benefits by exploiting their employees, their partners or people who have performed services for them, and have continued this unfair system for generations, families that have gained fame and fortune based on unjust practices.

Surprisingly, the spirit of injustice also operates in church organizations. This occurs when there is a hostile takeover of sorts, or when there is subversion against God's choice of leadership, such as a pastor. This spirit of injustice also works heavily within churches that were built under the guise of trickery or fraudulent propaganda, or even churches that operate under pastors who are bound by the spirit of injustice themselves.

This spirit is also seen operating in countries where parents allow their very young children to unwillingly marry a much older person just to obtain financial gains. In some cases, we have seen marriages between baby girls and grown men.

The spirit of injustice also operates in places where slavery is an open and active practice. These include countries where human beings are bought, sold, tortured or even murdered just because of their skin color, gender, nationality or faith.

We find ourselves asking questions like, "Why do awful things like these happen? What is the triggering factor that allows for this kind of behavior to occur? What is it that allows people who operate in these horrible practices, to lose their human sensibility?"

I am here to let you know that it was the revelation of the Holy Spirit in my life which directed me to see that all these evil dynamics were being caused by this evil spirit known as the spirit of injustice.

CHAPTER 3

Then we will no longer be infants, tossed back and forth by the waves, and blown here and there by every wind of teaching and by the cunning and craftiness of people in their deceitful scheming. (Eph. 4:14 NIV)

As I have mentioned before, this slimy spirit is extremely subtle in its modus operandi and not so detectable to the average believer. Many people, ministries, and nations don't even realize that they are under attack, or that they have been victims of this malignant spirit. They only see the end results of its destructive path, and are not able to perceive or identify its sneaky ministrations.

So we now know that the spirit of injustice can be assigned to nations, to ministries, to families, or even to individual lives. The ways in which the spirit of injustice could operate in one person's life are very diverse, but one way that is certain is through the manifestation of unjust cycles.

We also know that this spirit can operate through unstoppable chains of tragedies that seem to occur in incremental proportions. In other words, one is not completely free from a given problem when another tragedy begins, and so it continues. If this happens to us, it is vital that we recognize that we are being attacked by this evil spirit.

Examples of these attacks are people who are constant victims of injustices, or acts of injustice in their lives. People who invest everything in a relationship and receive no reciprocity in return. People who constantly strive for excellence at work and are never recognized for it.

Another example of being attacked by this spirit of injustice is being falsely accused. People that are imprisoned by the cycles of injustice are constantly being falsely accused, sued and even betrayed without reason by people they trust.

We can also see the manifestation of this evil spirit operating against a person when it steals their opportunities. For example, the job someone aspired to, that so much sacrifice was made to obtain, was then given to someone else.

This spirit also operates through abusers to people who have been sexually assaulted, or who have been through cycles of emotional or physical abuse, people who have gone through cycles of recurring divorces, abandonment, relationship failures and cycles of constantly being tricked or betrayed.

This slimy spirit also works to keep one from prospering economically, when so much effort has been dedicated to try and accomplish one's goals. These are people that never seem to reap the benefits of their hard work.

It seems like somehow the whole world has conspired against them. They feel stuck, like they can't advance in their lives, no matter how diligent or hard working they become, like they are constantly swimming against the current.

These people are the victims of constant cycles of losses. Every time they make a meaningful gain in their lives, it is partially lost, or in many cases it completely disappears. These people are often under cycles of financial leakages. Every time that person receives a financial benefit or payment, it is immediately dispersed because of some unforeseen emergency. For example, a person receives a bonus at work, but then his television breaks down and he needs to purchase another one. Or maybe his son has an accident and he needs to use that money for an emergency operation. Another example would be someone who received their dream watch, but then would have to resell or pawn it because of some unexpected emergency that occurred.

It is very important to note that all these events don't just happen at random. In fact, the cycles of injustice are what actually cause all these circumstances to occur over and over again. Yet we go on with life, unaware of that and withoutany logical explanation as to why these things keep happening to us.

Some more good examples are people that have never been appreciated in a relationship, no matter how much of an effort they make, people that have been abandoned for no apparent reason, and people who have always been loyal and truthful, and yet always fall victim to betrayals

We can also see the pattern of the spirit of injustice working through situations like sexual rape, even when the victim has taken all possible precautionary measures to avoid it.

We can also recognize the attack of this evil spirit through a lack of reciprocity: people who are always helping out others, but then receive unfair and bad behavior as their reward.

Here is a personal example of how this happened in my life. A few months after marrying my husband Ross, some behavioral patterns caught my attention. I was noticing how loyal and unselfish he was toward his friends, and how no one ever reciprocated his kindness and good heartedness.

I can remember that at the beginning of our marriage, one of Ross's best friends (we'll call him Tito to protect his identity) was going through some marital problems which eventually ended up in a divorce. My husband Ross, as the good friend that he was to Tito, decided to council him as much as he could through this very difficult situation, because there were children involved as well.

As soon as the divorce proceedings were finalized, Tito fell into a deep depression and Ross was there for him again.

One day, many months later, Tito decided to move to another city far away, and turn over the keys to his business, which included some very expensive factory equipment, to the landlord.

When Tito told Ross of his plan, Ross immediately sensed that Tito was making this hasty decision because of the emotional pain he was going through. Ross made Tito a generous deal, offering to pay the cost of the building rent, which would give Tito all the time he needed to heal emotionally and then return to work his business, which he was so good at doing.

Tito liked and agreed to the wonderful proposition my husband Ross had offered him. So everything was arranged and Tito went on his healing journey.

During the following year, Ross faithfully paid all the necessary bills of Tito's business, without receiving any assistance in return. After that year, Tito returned from his travels and Ross turned over the keys to him, noticing that Tito seemed to have recuperated from his emotional setbacks.

Then something really strange occurred. Tito gave Ross a quick thanks and went on his way to work in his business. Ross heard from Tito very rarely, and only when Ross would try and communicate with him. About another year went by with very little contact between Tito and Ross.

Then one day, Ross tried to contact Tito by phone, and received a message that the phone number had been disconnected. Ross then went directly to the workplace and found out that Tito had sold off the whole business, delivered the keys to the landlord and took off, without any notice to Ross, who had shown him true friendship.

Truly amazing, right?

Some time after this event, a similar situation occurred with the Pastor of a church we attended whom Ross helped out considerably and assisted like a brother. Ross even gave up his vehicle so that his wife could get around.

Ross and this pastor were so close that they would go to movies together, go scuba diving together and many other activities as well. Again, something interesting happened.

When the Pastor decided to end his contract with our church, he then moved back to his hometown and he never once called Ross.

These are just some of the unjust situations that have occurred in Ross's life, which have caught my attention. As many of you know, I am also a clinical psychologist. As such, I tried to analyze these situations several times. However, I finally came to the conclusion that this chain of unfair reciprocity that Ross was facing couldn't be explained by a simple emotional analysis, but that there were spiritual implications behind them.

I began noticing that these unjust occurrences surrounding our lives were happening more and more often, and each episode came on stronger than the previous one. We even had to shut down the family business, which then triggered a host of lawsuits. Thank God, none of them prospered and they were all adjudicated.

After winning all the court hearings and legal battles against a multitude of false accusations, I then found out that my husband was diagnosed with a severe health condition and he had to be operated on immediately!

During this whole difficult period of our lives, my husband and I maintained a stance of integrity before our God, and we kept ourselves deep in prayer.

It seemed as though our efforts weren't sufficient and that the devil himself was out to destroy our integrity and freedom. Even before Ross was able to recuperate from his critical surgery, we were hit with another barrage of bad news and lawsuits, all based on lies, trickery, false testimonies, and betrayals.

Yet, we were unaware of any rational reasons why all these attacks were coming our way and they seemed to have no end in sight. It wasn't until I began asking Ross about his past history that I was able to locate the root of the problem.

I found out that there was a negative event that fiercely marked Ross's life and left him filled with resentment, hatred, and a whole lot of vengeance in his heart. He could only live to think and plan out ways to take vengeance against those who committed the betrayals against him.

I then realized that this horrific betrayal that was perpetrated against Ross had activated the operation of the spirit of injustice, to attack him through a chain of a negative and unfair events.

Once my husband Ross yielded to the spirit of injustice, accepting the negative sentiments that it was ministering to his mind and emotions, Ross unconsciously opened the doors of his life and allowed this slimy spirit to exercise authority over him, through unjust cycles such as betrayal, unjust treatment, rejection, abuse and false testimonies,

This is what we identify as being under the oppressive attack of the spirit of injustice. It is when we open the door of our lives, consciously or unconsciously, to an evil spirit, allowing him to exercise authority over us. This also includes doors that our ancestors might have opened as well.

To be clear, an evil spirit can only exercise authority over us when we agree to yield our lives to its negative influences, or when we fall under its sinful practices.

But as I have said before, it's not that easy to perceive the presence of an evil spirit, and even harder to flush out the subtle operations of a slimy spirit, like the spirit of injustice. I need to add the fact that this evil spirit of injustice also works in association with other malignant spirits.

As I found it to be in our case, it was these cycles of injustice that were taking control of Ross's life, to the point that it was affecting the basic areas of our personal lives. It affected everything: our finances, our health, our ministry, our reputation, and even our daily activities.

The reason the spirit of injustice was able to also affect my life was because in the spiritual world, a married couple is considered to be one flesh. I too became a target of those unjust cycles, including losses in all areas of my life, envy, hatred, false testimonies and gossip.

Until one day we decided to wage spiritual warfare in favor of our deliverance, confessing our faults to God, asking for his forgiveness, and commanding the exodus of all those unjust spirits out of our lives, in the name of Jesus!

So, how does the spirit of injustice manage to be activated within a given family?

There are several causes that will activate the spirit of injustice on members of a given family. One of these ways is having been born into a family that already is operating under the influence of this sneaky spirit. In other words, through generational courses. That occurs when the head of a family, consciously or unconsciously, opens the door of his generation to a malignant spirit, through his sinful behaviors.

The spirit of injustice can also be activated in families that act or behave under the workings of this evil spirit. Families that are racially biased, that discriminate based on skin color, ethnicity, nationality, or social level.

This spirit can also have an open spiritual door in families that are abusive to their employees, making them work overtime and not paying them for it. Families that abuse people of lower income by taking away their property, etc.

We see it in families that commonly practice attitudes like being disloyal, hypocritical, judgmental, mocking, and ridiculing, families that feel comfortable practicing evil as if it were normal behavior. The mere fact that families operate in these kinds of evil ways opens the door to the spirit of injustice and gives it the legal right to operate through their generation.

This is how these demonic entities travel from generation to generation. Once a new generation begins to operate under the same evil parameters of the previous generation, a new cycle of generational curses begins, but this time it grows in strength and in scope.

In other words, each new generation inherits the previous sinful behaviors, but then the newer generation not only develops stronger behavioral patterns, but also adds on more related evil spirits, thus multiplying the intensity of the evil within the family genealogy.

It will require that a member of this family that has received Jesus in his or her heart, confesses to God the sins of the family, asks God for forgiveness, and cancels those generational curses, in the name of Jesus! However, having said this, the task of breaking generational curses is not an easy one. Let's not forget that the minute an evil spirit realizes that someone is trying to break away from its grip, those spirits will begin a relentless attack against them.

The family member that wants to turn to Christ, must be really firm in their desire to cast out all those evil spirits, in the name of Jesus! After casting these evil spirits out from their lives, they must begin learning about how to operate under the parameters that rule the kingdom of God.

How does this spirit of injustice manage to enter the life of a person?

The spirit of injustice can enter the life of a person through a traumatic experience caused by someone who is under the influence of this slimy spirit. (Much like the example I have mentioned regarding my husband Ross.)

Other examples can be seen in people who have been victims of sexual assault and abuse, or people who have suffered cycles of humiliation, abandonment and betrayals.

More examples can be found in people who have been forced into practices against their moral principles and desires. This terrible spirit can also be activated in the life of a person by means of pacts, which might also have been made unconsciously.

As I have mentioned before, as the body of Christ, we often get involved in doing what everyone else is doing, forgetting the fact that we have been specially chosen and that we are part of God's sacred nation.

This means that we cannot participate in some of the mundane customs and family cultures that are in conflict with God's Word. If we decide to partake in these types of activities, then we are at risk of falling into this world of unjust behaviors.

Through these unsavory practices, we then open the doors of our lives, and align ourselves to operate in sync with all the evil spirits associated with those sinful practices.

Often when we open these doors, we are opening them up unconsciously, making "unconscious pacts." In other words, unconscious pacts are the ones that open the doors to our lives so that these evil spirits can minister and influence the decision-making process of our lives.

Eventually, these sneaky spirits begin to take over all of our decisions with the authority they have, and they start wreaking havoc, chaos, confusion and destruction. In the case of the spirit of injustice, it will provoke unjust events in all different areas of our lives.

CHAPTER 4

As I have mentioned before, the spirit of injustice can also be activated in an entire given country or nation. There are several ways this can happen. This is often accomplished through the forceful taking of land masses, death of the innocent dwellers of the land taken, and stealing everything in sight. These nations have been formed and have grown under the force of unjust cycles.

We can also observe these unjust cycles working in countries that are governed by a dictator. We all know that in any true dictatorship, there's an overwhelming abuse of power, intimidation of the people, fraudulent elections and much more. Countries or nations that do not look to change their dictatorial ways and turn toward the almighty God, with a more equitable and just political system, are doomed to fail, precisely because of the destructive nature of the spirit of injustice.

There are also countries that have strong ties to idolatry and have, as their religious foundation, practices of occultism. This may include rituals related to witchcraft, sorcery, santeria and may have even consecrated their whole nation to a divinity of the occult.

We can see unjust cycles working in nations that actively practice racism and where human rights and the benefits of just laws only go to those who can pay for them. There are also nations that pose a culture of gossip, where the main objective is to diminish and destroy the good name and reputation of others.

You also have nations where "machismo" is predominant; where women, children and the elderly are worth nothing and often even considered expendable.

What is important to note here is that all of these situations feed and nourish these unjust spirits, which have been assigned to these nations for the sole purpose of confounding the minds of their citizens, so as to keep them spiritually bound.

Every time a citizen operates under the unjust parameters that are ruling his nation, the evil spirit becomes stronger, and its influence continues to be reinforced in the minds of the subsequent generations of that nation. In other words, every citizen that allows the spirit of injustice to operate in their lives automatically reinforces those unjust cycles, and actively maintains them within that nation by being willful collaborators to those evil spirits.

Someone who allows this system of injustice to operate in them has made an unconscious alliance with this evil spirit, whether or not they are aware they're doing so. They have also failed to realize the fact that they have opened the door of their life to this evil spirit, thus giving it the freedom to operate in any area of their lives.

Once I could identify this slimy spirit, I began to see more clearly, and have continued to be intrigued by peculiar observations during and after the production of this book.

I see the way this spirit of injustice is working in Latin American countries and in some of the Caribbean Islands. The reason so many of these populations are trying to immigrate into the United States is that most of these Spanish-speaking countries are operating under corruption, which is one of the sinful practices that opens the spiritual door of a nation to this evil spirit.

However, when these people arrive in the States, even though they are in a country of just laws, they continue to be the object of abuse. Unless they rebuke this spirit, it will maintain its hold on them. They must decide to cast them out, in the name of Jesus.

Another great example of this can be found in the African American community of the United States. Even though slavery has been abolished for many years, we still see how the black community is struggling to get ahead, or even occupy meaningful positions in our society.

The reason for this continuing racial disparity is that there are so many generations of this spirit of injustice that still need to be rebuked. So even though slavery has been legally abolished in most parts of the world, that doesn't mean the spirit of injustice has been completely defeated.

If we don't properly rebuke the spirit of injustice, it will remain in its legal domain and it will continue to exercise authority over the people or nations that have opened their doors and let it in.

By now some of you have probably asked yourselves the obvious follow up question: If the United States came into existence by violent war, the taking of land masses and by the shedding of so much blood, why isn't the spirit of injustice hovering over it and its people in a stronger way?

Well, I will give you the same answer that the Holy Spirit gave me when I asked him this question. All the bloodshed, violence and murder that occurred while the American nation was being formed absolutely *did* open up the doors to the spirit of injustice.

We know of many historical events that happened in the days of the Wild West, where the law was in the hands of the fastest gun slingers or the more astute killers. In other words, there was no law in those days and everything was reducedto the survival of the fittest.

It wasn't until this newly formed nation turned their hearts back to the Lord, and decided to officially put God first, in their constitution, on their currency, and even in their presidential elections, that they could stem the tide of wicked influence and operation of the spirit of injustice over the USA.

> If my people, who call my name, will humble themselves and pray and seek my face and turn from their wicked ways, then will I hear from heaven and will forgive their sin and will heal their land. (2 Chron. 7: 14 NIV)

Since the inception of the United States of America, it has been the custom to elect a president with basic Judeo-Christian principles and to honor our God by placing their right hand on the Bible while they are being sworn into office.

Because of this culture of honoring God in everything, God has honored the United States by placing this nation as the first world economic and military power.

> God honors those who honor him. (1 Sam. 2:30)

We can see that as the United States began to bring back the government of God to the country, the spirit of injustice that had such a strong grip on it, had to run away and release its oppression and stronghold over the whole nation.

This resulted in a systematic reduction of the spirit of slavery, unjust land grabs, and murders of black Americans. Slowly but surely, laws were established that were fair and just for everyone.

I don't mean to say that the States are completely free of this slimy spirit. There will always be a residual factor that remains hovering around in "dry places." What I can affirm is that because the United States decided to put God first in all of these areas, this allowed the nation to be free from the oppression of this deplorable spirit.

Let me explain. It is not the same thing to be under the *influence* of this scummy spirit, as it is to be under its *oppression*.

To be under the influence of a spirit is to be tempted, or lured, or even attracted to that spirit, and have with them the intentions of participating in their devious practices.

In contrast, when we are under the oppression of a malignant spirit, this means that a person actually operates under an evil system which has already been previously established. The person must be obedient and follow all the rules and regulations that bind them to that spirit. In other words, the person is completely subjected to its authority.

To be more specific, there are countries whose laws, culture, social and political systems, its defining religion, and even its popular perceptions and ideologies, are governed by very unjust concepts. In other words, these nations accept,support and normalize the practices of an unjust and unequal society.

I'm referring to countries that are not outraged by seeing an eight year old pregnant girl, that was the result of a family member raping her. I'm referring to countries where human trafficking is a legitimate business venture and no one even questions it.

I'm referring to countries that find it a common occurrence to hear the frantic screams of a woman being physically attacked by her spouse, and nobody comes to help her because it's considered normal behavior.

I'm referring to countries that purposely don't offer decent medical assistance to their poor and where children are dying daily for lack of clean water. We define these countries as being under the oppression of the spirit of injustice.

Let's look back at the United States for a moment. The Bible teaches us that when a malignant spirit is expelled from a territory, it lingers over "dry places," just waiting for another opportunity to re-enter that territory.

This should cause a major red alert to America, even though it has shown great respect for God, and even though it has developed one of the greatest justice systems in the world.

All these accomplishments have reflected a huge victory over the spirit of injustice and its government. However, this could easily change or be threatened if the States were to decide to turn away from the Christian principles that made the country so remarkable in the first place.

We have begun to see the systematic elimination of God from our public school systems, the cancellation of public praying at public sporting events, the removal of Bibles from hotel and motel rooms, the omission of swearing on the Bible in court rooms and even blatant disrespect toward men and women of the cloth.

It was also extremely threatening for America to have elected a president that wasn't an active and practicing Christian, but in reality practiced a pagan religion whose origin is from countries that are under the oppression of the spirit of injustice. This created the perfect atmosphere for the return of this slimy spirit back into the country.

We can only imagine what catastrophic events might have happened if the United States had not chosen a God-fearing president for the 2016 White House. It could have meant some giant steps backwards for the nation. It might have even reopened the doors to the spirit of injustice, and the results would have been monumentally worse!

If we want to keep America on a godly track, as its citizens, we must make it our mission to ensure that we do everything we can to uphold the Judeo-Christian principles which made it so great to begin with.

Let me be very clear. I am using the nation of the United States of America to show you how the spirit of injustice can be cast out of a country just as easily as it can also return to it, if that country were to turn away from God and His principles.

The spirit of injustice can also infiltrate and become activated in churches and ministries. This may be caused by several factors, including when a ministry has been founded through unjust acts or intentions. For example, the church council deciding to unjustly remove the founder, or pastor, in order to place someone else. This could also occur when people form a new church at the expense of another, or give false testimonies and criticisms against the pastor, and then form a new group based on this deception. The unjust spirit also takes hold when pastors wrongfully take riches from their church members to supply the needs of their ministries.

The spirit of injustice can also infiltrate a ministry through ministerial stagnancy. We see this when a pastor is living a Godly life and is dedicated to the ministry, but his church has no meaningful growth or advancements. In these cases, it can seem as though the more the members work at trying to advance the growth of the church, the more it remains at a standstill.

This could well be because of the spirit of injustice has taken a position over that particular territory and has kept its grip on it. Or it is also possible that this slick spirit has been assigned to the pastor, or to the family's name, in order to wage war against them.

In any one of these cases, the key to getting rid of these slimy spirits is to renounce and rebuke them in the name of Jesus. This is the way you permanently remove their authority to operate in your life or your ministry.

Another way this scummy spirit can slither into a church setting is through a pastor's preferential treatment of his or her members; when a leader is more interested in the social status of particular churchgoers than their heart for service, ordedication to the church program and vision.

My husband Ross and I witnessed firsthand this exact circumstance, and the experience became the triggering factor that the Holy Spirit used to unleash the truth about this horrific spirit of injustice.

We came to visit a particular church because they had invited a gospel singer to perform that we really enjoyed listening to. Just before the guest singer began his repertoire, he announced that he would like to give away one of his most recent CD's to a member of the public.

Guess who he gave this CD to? None other than the most elegant and wealthy couple in the church, who were always specially seated in the very front row facing the podium.

Fortunately, my husband and I were sitting right behind this couple and we were able to observe the whole process. It just so happens that the church was full to capacity that night and they were mostly from the more humble levels of the working class. Many of them would have loved to receive the CD of the vocalist, and likely could not afford to purchase it themselves.

I then noticed an elderly lady, whom I had always made an effort to greet, and who was a faithful attendee at all the services, despite the fact that she couldn't drive and had to come by bus. I thought to myself, "Wouldn't it have been marvelous if this elderly woman were the one to have received the CD?"

I couldn't explain why, but that seemingly insignificant event stuck in my head for a long time. I finally went to the Holy Spirit and asked him, "Why do things like this happen in the house of God? Why do we as believers, seem to operate under the same set of values as the rest of the world?"

It was at that very moment that the Holy Spirit spoke to me and revealed that it was actually the spirit of injustice which was operating in all those unfair events. It was then that the Holy Spirit revealed this evil spirit and how it manages to operate on earth.

Now, I was able to better understand the dynamics surrounding the actions of the vocalist. You see, the singer is originally from a country whose government operates under a heavy-handed dictatorship, and whose larger population is enslaved by the people in power. Having lived under this kind of political oppression for most of his life, he had retained this spirit of injustice with him, and he carried it without even knowing he was doing so.

What most often occurs in churches that are under this spirit of injustice is, soberingly, considered very ordinary. This is when it invades our churches by common behaviors including gossip, rebellion, conflict, poverty, absenteeism, lack of prosperity and a noticeable difference in social status. All this chaos and confusion causes the members of the church to feel underappreciated, which fuels a ferocious atmosphere to seek status or positions of power.

CHAPTER 5

B ut he said, "Your brother came deceitfully and took your blessing." (Gen. 27:35 NIV)

As I have mentioned before, the reason God sent his son to this earth was mainly to redeem us from sin. However, we also understand that God's even deeper objective was to do this by reversing the cycles of injustice, social inequality and our sinful ways, and in the process, establish his kingdom of love, compassion, social equality and justice for all.

In other words, this fight against the spirit of injustice is nothing new. In fact, it has existed since the beginning of time. When we take a closer look at biblical times, we see that many of God's people were under the attack of, or influenced by, the spirit of injustice.

Let's take a look at Genesis 27, where we read the story of how Jacob steals the inheritance of the first born from his brother, Esau.

As many of you know, the blessing on the first born was an important prayer, rich in benefits, given to the eldest son by the father before his (the father's) death. This special prayer is known as the "patriarchal blessing."

The story tells us that when it was time for Isaac to give the patriarchal blessing to his eldest son Esau, Jacob conspired (with his mother, Rebecca) to steal this blessing for himself.

We can observe how the spirit of injustice persuaded both Jacob and his mother to commit unjust acts through lies, fraud and trickery. Jacob's fraudulent and unjust acts opened the door to the spirit of injustice, which actively operated in his life, right up until his death.

It's entirely possible that Rebecca didn't even know that she was under the influence of this spirit. In fact, she might have thought that all she was doing was helping the son she favored the most receive the patriarchal blessing. We can also speculate that she, most likely, didn't realize the enormous damage she would be causing to her family.

We could also surmise that Rebecca had allowed the spirit of injustice into her life on other occasions. We know that the mere fact Rebecca was favoring her son Jacob over his other siblings was itself an act of injustice. So Rebecca already had an open door for the spirit of injustice to enter her life.

This is precisely the way the spirit of injustice operates, through common, everyday events that seem normal or even advantageous. Often, this slimy spirit even persuades us to partake in its evil workings, involving the people we love and who are dear to our hearts, as in the case of Jacob and Rebecca.

To be clear, Jacob yielded to the ministrations of the spirit of injustice when he tricked his father into believing that he was actually his brother, Esau. This was an elaborate scheme, meant to trick his blind father into giving him the patriarchal blessing instead of his older brother, Esau.

Another item that needs clarification is the fact that just because we have been offered to open the door to the spirit of injustice, doesn't mean that it can automatically begin operations. We actually open the door ourselves, once we yield to its temptation.

In other words, it's not the mere temptation that is the sin which allows the spirit of injustice to take over one's life, but rather it is our response to that temptation that either opens or shuts that door.

In the Bible, we read of when Jesus was tempted in the wilderness, but he never gave in and sinned (Heb. 4:5). Temptations are a part of our lives, as well as our walk with God. This is why Jesus instructed His disciples to pray continuously, so as to not fall into temptation (Matt. 26:41).

When we yield to temptation, we are giving the enemy the legal right to exercise dominion over us, when it should be the exact opposite. You see, as servants of God, we have actually been given the authority to exercise dominion over all things created. However, every time we fall into sin, we relinquish that authority and we open the door to our lives, giving the enemy the power to exercise its authority over us.

How did the spirit of injustice operate throughout Jacob's life?

As I have said before, once we yield to the persuasion, or temptation, of this scummy spirit of injustice, we open the doors, consciously, or unconsciously, to operate in our lives. This is precisely what happened in the life of Jacob.

Biblical history tells us that shortly after he had tricked his father and his older brother, Jacob had to fight the angel for his rights to the blessing (Gen. 32:24 NIV).

In other words, Jacob had to fight for something that was already his. This begs the question that if Jacob's father had already blessed him, and that blessing is irrevocable, then why did Jacob had to fight the angel for it all over again?

This is actually a common result of those who are operating under the oppression of the spirit of injustice. It always takes them twice as much effort to reach their blessings and accomplish their goals.

Every endeavor that they try to achieve will inevitably become twice as difficult as it would be for someone who is not under the influence of this slimy spirit. What takes a truly free person only one year to accomplish, will take two or more years for someone under this influence. They find themselves facing great difficulties to be successful or even find prosperity in their lives. Every time they attempt to obtain something big in their lives, it falls completely apart before it can be manifested.

Sometimes, people under the influence of this slimy spirit, will show the consequences of their struggles in their bodies and illnesses. Take for instance Jacob, who ended up limping for the rest of his life because of the injury he suffered while fighting the angel for his blessing.

A second example of injustice that Jacob faced was when he had to work twice as hard to obtain his marriage to Rachel, the woman that he truly loved (Gen. 29 NIV).

The Bible tells us that Jacob had to flee the persecution of his brother, Esau. His mother, Rebecca, instructed him to go and stay at her brother Laban's house. Jacob did so, and after a short time, he fell in love with his uncle's youngest daughter, Rachel. When Jacob confessed his love for Rachel to his uncle Laban, he agreed to work for Laban for seven years, in return for her hand in marriage.

After the seven years had been fulfilled, Laban tricked Jacob into marrying his older daughter, Leah. When Jacob realized the switch, he went back to claim Rachel. His uncle then demanded another seven years of labor in order to finally marry Rachel.

This was completely unjust behavior on the part of Laban, because this wasn't the original bargain, and to make it even more unfair, Jacob had kept up his side of the deal, fair and square. This is just another common example of how the spirit of injustice works to oppress the lives of all the people who have allowed it to control them. No matter how hard they work, they just don't seem to be able to get ahead, see the fruits of their labor, or receive what has been promised to them, even when they've rightfully earned it. In other words, the more they drive themselves to succeed, the further away they get from their purpose.

These people have to work double for anything they want, and Jacob is a prime example. Even after receiving a double portion of the blessing, it wasn't enough to stifle the consequences of opening the door to the spirit of injustice.

Another unjust episode in the life of Jacob occurred when he finally got to marry Rachel. He then found out that she was unable to bear children. In other words, even after Jacob worked a total of fourteen years to marry the love of his life and to finally start a family of his own, he was unable to see his dream come true.

Bringing sterility to people is another way the spirit of injustice slithers into our lives, begins to operate, and exerts authority. This includes sterility in our finances, spiritual sterility, mental sterility (which can be seen through a lack of creativity), and yes, physical reproductive sterility.

Strictly speaking, when we open the door to the spirit of injustice, we are letting it operate in the areas of poverty, spiritual stagnancy, stagnancy in our ministry and loss of the ability to be productive. We are constantly being attacked through its powers of causing droughts, scarcity and a general stoppage of any advancements in our lives.

Another example of how the spirit of injustice had a direct affect on the life of Jacob, was through the false accusations that were made against him.

> Jacob has taken everything our father owned and has gained all this wealth from what belonged to our father. (Gen. 31:1 NIV)

After all that Jacob had gone through, his many sacrifices, his hard work and the abusive treatment he received from his uncle Laban, Jacob finally managed to prosper. His possessions and his livestock were multiplied.

But when Jacob's cousins found out about all of his successes, they began a smear campaign against Jacob, claiming he had taken advantage of Laban's wealth and trust. Of course, this was all false, but Jacob was still forced to flee.

These things often accompany people that have allowed the spirit of injustice to oppress their lives. They can experience false accusations, inexplicable rejections and hatred from people who don't bother to investigate the truth about them.

Having said all this, it is also very common for people under the oppressive influence of the spirit of injustice to not realize what is happening to them and why are they on the receiving end of so many attacks. They are perplexed at the fact that no matter how hard they try to please people, nothing seems to work in their favor.

That is why it is so important to learn the correct strategies on how to identify this sick spirit, so we can avoid its slimy web. And if we find that we have fallen into its web, we need to educate ourselves on how to rebuke its operations and influences over our lives.

We continue to see this deplorable spirit affecting Jacob's life, and each problem that he had to endure seemed to be worse than the previous one. We see this happening when we find out that Rachel, the love of Jacob's life, ended up dying at a relatively young age.

This is yet another way the scummy spirit of injustice works to destroy our lives, through tragedies such as sudden and unexpected deaths, suicides, incurable illnesses, divorces, destruction, and more cycles of loss.

I would like to share an experience I had in one of the churches that my parents gave pastoral guidance to. There was a young prayer leader at this church, who we will call Lala, who became an orphan at a very young age. Lala had two older sisters who decided to take on the role of Lala's parents. Even though the older sisters began to work, things were so bad financially that they both decided to supplement their income by becoming ladies of the night.

After just a few years, both sisters fell victim to an incurable disease and died, leaving little Lala an orphan for the second time. Before reaching the legal age, Lala married a very kind gentleman, who loved and respected her very much.

It is at this juncture of their lives, that they decided to join our church. Over the next few years, the Lord blessed this couple with three children, one daughter and two sons. By now, Lala's husband had turned into one of the leading musicians at our church.

Lala's husband began to suffer from strong abdominal pains, and informed Lala that he was going to use some homemade remedies that a local lady prepared for people, and he went to her home. After several hours had passed, Lala became very worried and decided to call the police.

Lala gave the officers all the details of her husband and this lady, The police had heard of this local woman before, and in fact, had enough evidence to obtain a search warrant and interrogate this "medicine woman" at her home. The officers made a grim discovery there. Lifting up one of the beds, they found the body of Lala's husband, wrapped in plastic. The medicine lady claimed that it was an involuntary reaction to the home remedy that she gave Lala's husband. After further investigation, however, the officers found out that Lala's husband wasn't the first victim of the lady's "remedies."

Time passed, and eventually Lana fell in love again and remarried. He was a wonderful man who also attended our church, and it seemed Lana would finally get to enjoy life free of the tragedies that plagued her. A year into their marriage however, Lala received devastating news yet again. Her second husband had suffered a terrible motorcycle accident. After several days in the ICU, he passed away as well.

Lala decided to spend the next few years seeking refuge and spiritual strength by actively participating in our church through praise and prayer. One day, Lala was directing the church choir, praising the Lord, and having a wonderful time in front of the congregation. Suddenly, the music stopped. It looked as though Lala was laying down on the floor. Everyone thought that Lala was under some sort of spiritual trance. However, when she didn't get up, someone went to check her pulse. Inexplicably, abruptly and without warning, she had died.

The church made the decision to adopt Lala's four children and provide for all of their needs. Shortly thereafter, the church was informed that one of Lala's underage daughters was pregnant, and months later, gave birth to a beautiful baby girl.

Even after Lala's death, the tragedy that seemed to define her life continued with her children, as the church received even more devastating news. Lala's daughter, a new mother herself, had contracted HIV at only 19 years old.

(As I write these words, I am glad to report that the young mother is recuperating in the hospital. Unfortunately, due to weakness, transfusions and the physical stress of the illness, she lost her baby in the ordeal.) It truly seems as though the cycle of tragedy in this family is never ending!

It was this example, as well as numerous others, that brought me to ask the Holy Spirit, "Why so much tragedy in one single family? Why are innocent babies and children exposed to such pain and suffering? Why did Lala, the church leader of prayer and worship, have to be the recipient of such a long chain of tragic events, and why do her children have to suffer the continuing cycles of catastrophic tragedy and loss?"

Finally, it was revealed to me that all these people were under the operating force of the spirit of injustice, through doors opened in the present, or that had been opened in their past. The most important thing about my revelation is that it showed me the sequence of events that we could use to cancel out and finally stop these evil spirits of injustice.

The Holy Spirit showed me how we must rebuke the generational curses that have been operating throughout family members and generations, never forgetting that it must be done in the name of Jesus Christ!

We clearly see this spirit of injustice working its influence throughout the life of Jacob, when it took the young life of his wife, Rachel. We also see how this slimy spirit continued working within the family's lineage when Jacob's older sons decided to kidnap and even sell their younger brother, Joseph, because they were envious of him.

The trickery that Jacob's sons played on him caused him so many years of grief. The story begins when Joseph's older brothers decided to actually kill him, but failed in their attempt. As some merchants happened to be passing through the region, it dawned on them that they could sell their brother as a slave, ridding themselves of him forever. The brothers then returned home and told their father, Jacob, that Joseph was devoured by a wild lion (Gen. 37:31).

I hope you all can appreciate the irony of what took place in the storyline of this family history. Isn't it curious how Jacob was tricked into believing that his younger son had been devoured by a lion, just as Jacob had tricked his own father into believing that he was the eldest son, Esau, in order to receive the patriarchal blessing?

Again, we can clearly see how the cycle of trickery, fraud and lies, are transferred from one generation to the next. This is precisely how this scummy spirit of injustice travels from generation to generation until someone in the family chain decides to rebuke it in the name of Jesus!

We can go back even further into the life of Jacob, and we read the story where at birth, Jacob held the heel of his twin brother to try to come out first. We may even ask ourselves how it is that while still in the womb of his mother, Jacob had the consciousness to know what to try do in order to get in front of his twin brother (Gen. 25: 19-34).

In the spirit world, the answer is actually very basic. These spirits are transferred through generational curses. It could be that one of our ancestors had opened a door to one of these evil spirits and have since continued to operate in the family for generations.

It's also entirely possible that the spirit of injustice had already been influencing the lives of Rebecca, Jacob's mother, and Laban, Jacob's uncle. So it would be pretty accurate to say that Jacob was born into a family that was already beingactively used by the spirit of injustice. Thus, Jacob inherited these slimy spirits from his mother's side, and then he passed them on to his sons, and so on and so on.

One might also deduce from all this information that if the spirit of injustice operates through lies, trickery, and manipulation, then it is also logical to assume that we all have been stricken by the influence, or persuasions, of this spirit of injustice! Well, you are absolutely correct! This is why it is so important to come before the Lord every day, and confess your sins, rebuke the evil workings of these dark spirits and ask to be forgiven, in the name of Jesus Christ.

Jesus taught his disciples to pray the Lord's Prayer, and it is our best example of how we all should pray on a daily basis. This prayer teaches us to enter into the Lord's presence by praising Him, worshipping Him and exalting Him. Then, to confess our sins to Him.

However, we are making a big mistake when we confess to God only when we have committed a "large sin," and not what we might consider minor, such as "white lies," or tricking or manipulate someone. The fact is, this is precisely what the spirit of injustice is looking for, so it can take advantage over our lives and begin its slimy operations. It is God's Word that teaches us to not fall into temptation, so if we focus on that, the spirit of injustice will have no power over our lives.

> But the cowardly, the unbelieving, the vile, the murderers, the sexually immoral, those who practice magic arts, the idolaters and all the liars,

their place will be in the fiery lake of burning
sulfur. This is the second death. (Rev. 21:8 NIV)

I find it very interesting how God has placed the "big sins"
(murders, adultery and witchcraft) right along with the "smaller
sins" (lying and cowardliness), as if there wasn't a difference in
magnitude between the sins.

The reason God makes no exceptions to sinning, is because
all sins represent a direct threat to our spiritual lives and the
salvation of our souls. All sins, big or small, open the door to
the enemy so it can exercise authority over our lives.

This is why many times we are tempted to think that the
small sins won't do any noticeable harm, when actually, these
small sins begin to expand into much larger situations. That,
in fact, takes away our authority and blocks the answers to our
petitions and blessings. Again, we can use the life story of Jacob
to demonstrate this concept.

I hope I've made it clear enough so that everyone is able
to understand all the dynamics of how this scummy spirit
of injustice actually infiltrates our lives and our family's
genealogical roots. Hopefully, we are now able to better
recognize the many different facets of these generational spirits
of injustice working in the life of Jacob. He remains a very good
example because of all the things he had to go through. He was
sold by his own brothers. He was imprisoned for something
he didn't do when he was falsely accused of rape by Potiphar's
wife. He had finally managed to prosper and gain a position
of honor, only to have everything turn against him and lose it
all at once.

The fact that Jacob was under the influence of the spirit
of injustice doesn't mean that God didn't use him to fulfill
his purpose. It was just the many struggles and inexplicable
tragedies that Jacob had to endure to get there. Well, this is how
the spirit of injustice works, by lengthening our pathway to

our blessings, and by multiplying our struggles and difficulties along the way to our destiny.

When we are being attacked by the spirit of injustice, we get the feeling that we are walking backward and not forward. Everything is delayed and we don't get to accomplish any of our projects. Again, it feels as though we are being blocked by a huge wall of concrete. In other words, it's as though we still fall short of our expectations after we have put so much effort, time and dedication into the completion of our goals.

CHAPTER 6

It doesn't matter how the spirit of injustice filters into our lives. The one fact that remains constant is that once it has taken over our lives, its purpose is to cause catastrophes and destruction there.

> The thief comes only to steal and kill and destroy; I have come that they may have life, and have it to the full. (John 10:10 NIV)

Let's take a look at another well-known biblical figure who was also over taken by this slimy spirit of injustice, and was visibly influenced and attacked by it. We know him to be David's son Solomon.

The story begins in 2 Samuel 11, when King David was walking the grounds of his palace, and stumbled upon a beautiful maiden taking a bath. King David was mesmerized by her beauty, and asked one of his servants to find out who she was. His servant returned with the intel that the beautiful lady was the wife of David's most trusted army general, the mighty warrior Uriah. Knowing this, David still summoned Bathsheba to him, and ended up getting her pregnant.

King David then conjured up a plan to invite the couple to the palace, in hopes that he could stimulate their romantic desires, thus being able to naturally shift the cause for Bathsheba's pregnancy on Uriah, her rightful husband. Instead,

Uriah chose to stand guard in the palace so he could protect his king. This is how faithful and devoted he was to King David, a loyalty which seems to be extremely scarce today.

Nevertheless, King David finally devised a way to avoid the discovery of his sin with Bathsheba. He decided to send Uriah to the front lines of the battle field, purposely placing him in direct danger to be killed (2 Sam. 11:15). Everything went according to King David's plan. Uriah went to the front lines of the battle and was killed. After Bathsheba heard the news, she mourned her husband's death. Once her period of mourning had passed, King David summoned Bathsheba to the palace and made her his wife.

We could look at this story and think that everything turned out perfect for King David, but when you open the door for the spirit of injustice to begin its influence, make no mistake about it, the consequences turn out to be catastrophic. It doesn't matter how close we think we are to the heart of the Lord (like King David was), or how often we go to church, or even how many Psalms we can memorize, the consequences of allowing any malignant spirit to minister and influence our lives, are inevitable.

The fact that King David committed that horrible act against his most trusted general definitely opened the door to the spirit of injustice and allowed it to "set up shop" in the life of King David and all his descendants. We see how this slimy spirit of injustice operates through tragedies and cycles of injustice, throughout King David's life and that of his descendants.

The first calamity that happened to King David after he opened the door to these evil spirits, was that his newborn son, the one that was the result of his sinful relationship with Bathsheba, died at birth (2 Sam. 12:15-17).

The second calamity that happened to the King was that his eldest son, Amnon, planned and executed the rape of his own sister, Tamar. Amnon then had the audacity to publicly repudiate Tamar (2 Sam. 13:17).

The third calamity that occured in King David's life is when another one of his sons, Absalom, conspired to kill Amnon, in revenge for raping and defiling Tamar (2 Sam. 13:28).

After these tragic events fell upon King David, Absalon began to show tremendous disdain for his father and becomes his father's worst enemy (2 Sam. 15). We can observe how the spirit of injustice slithered into King David's life without his knowledge, and how it systematically destroyed everything surrounding his life and that of his family. This pattern of tragic events followed King David all the way to his grave.

The bloodshed and grotesque actions that occurred in King David's house laid so heavily upon it, that God himself said to David that he could not build his Temple, because there was too much blood on David's hands (1 Chron. 22:8). However, we can also see King David's genuine desire to get rid of the terrible cycle of tragedy that had taken over his life and the lives of his beloved family members (1 Chron. 22:8).

In Psalm 51:14, we read that King David truly wanted to free himself of these overpowering evil spirits that had taken over his household. Again, this is what can happen when we allow these slippery spirits of injustice to enter our lives and take control.

It is vitally important to remember that these evil spirits don't just appear out of nowhere, but are a direct consequences of doors that we have opened, or an indirect consequence of doors opened through our family lineage, or even from an established influence that hovers over our nation. It is not due to laziness, negligence or irresponsibility that would justify these events, and it's not like we can flip a switch and make them disappear.

The root of it all stems from the spiritual faults that we often aren't even aware of having indulged. This ignorance come from the very stealthy way it enters into our lives. As I have mentioned before, many of the temptations that help open the doors to these scummy spirits are very hard to identify or detect.

This is why I want to make sure that you are able to grasp the concept of how sneaky this spirit of injustice really is, and how difficult it is to know when you are under its influence and attacks. We often face these trials and simply end up asking things like, "What is happening to my life? Why is everything so hard? Why is everything I do so difficult for me to accomplish?"

I must take this opportunity to clarify how we can identify this spirit of injustice and when we are under its oppression or attacks, and not simply mistake it for the times that our bad situation is actually our fault. These things might have merely occurred as a product of bad or negligent decisions we have made for our lives.

That said, it doesn't totally eliminate the possibility of these spirits coexisting with each other, causing their combined influence to interact in our lives as a direct product of our negligent decisions and behaviors.

When this happens, the results are very similar to if they were acting independently, and their consequences reflect a fairly similar negative impact on our lives. It basically doesn't allow you to grow spiritually and therefore keeps you from advancing and prospering in your own life.

What we can be sure of is that once we have allowed the spirit of injustice to establish itself in our lives, we are then submerged in a series of events and attacks that can include betrayal, insurrection, hatred, and the like, without it being consciously provoked by us. This is very much like what happened in the life of King David.

> Ruthless witnesses come forward; they question me on things I know nothing about. They repay me evil for good and leave my soul forlorn. (Psalms 35:11-12 NIV)

In this Bible passage, King David gives us a clear description of what the spirit of injustice actually does in our lives. It provokes the insurrection of evil witnesses to rise up and spew false testimonies against us. Another way that these evil spirits operate is through acts of trickery that are intended to make us vulnerable and fail. King David clearly said, "They question me on things I know nothing about" (Psalms 35:11 NIV).

In this passage, "they" refers to people that only place themselves in our lives for the explicit purpose of creating a false narrative against us. Again, this is similar to what was happening to King David, who was being severely attacked by his enemies without any apparent provocation or cause. Whether David knew it or not, he wasn't just being attacked by his human enemies, but ultimately by these slimy spirits of injustice.

King David was also besieged by unjust retribution, and we see this in verse 12 when he says, "They repay me evil for good and leave my soul forlorn" (Psalms 35:12 NIV). When we are under attack by these evil spirits of injustice, we are never properly compensated for our efforts. In fact, quite the opposite happens. In King David's case, he was being unjustly abused in terrible payback by the very people he had helped.

We also see how King David was attacked by these evil spirits through the many betrayals that he had to suffer.

> And when they were ill, I put on sackcloth and humbled myself with fasting. When my prayers returned to me unanswered, I went about mourning as though for my friend or brother. I bowed my head in grief as though weeping for my mother. But when I stumbled, they gathered in glee; attackers gathered against me when I was unaware. They slandered me without ceasing."
> (Psalms 35:13-15 NIV)

We can see from these verses that King David was feeling distraught and betrayed by the people he had played for, fasted for and humbled himself with sackcloth for, just to show his solidarity in their time of need. Further, these were people he considered brothers. Yet, they returned David's good deeds with hatred, betrayal of his genuine friendship and unjustified bad attitudes, and "when [he] stumbled, they gathered with glee" (Psalms 35: 15 NIV).

Another very distinct method that the spirit of injustice used against King David was the fact that he was unaware of where the attacks were coming from, and why they were really happening.

> Attackers gathered against me when I was unaware. (Psalms 35:15 NIV)

It is very common for people who are under attack of the spirit of injustice to not be aware of the root reasons that these negative events keep happening to them. Often, these people simply end up thinking things like, "I simply don't have any luck at all! I have never been able to accomplish anything and the little I do have has taking me forever to obtain. I am always overlooked, and exhausted with trying so hard. I just can't catch a break. I don't see any light at the end of the tunnel."

It is obvious that people under attack know that something terrible is happening to them, and feel like they should be further ahead, but can't get a good explanation why, and are completely unaware that they are under the attack of a malignant spirit. As King David expressed, he didn't have a clue where all these tragedies were coming from.

We can compare this to harvesting a crop. Very simply put, you can't plant corn and expect to reap potatoes. So, when we are under attack of the spirit of injustice, what we receive is the exact opposite of what we have worked for in our accomplishments, or given to in our relationships with others.

For example, when people return evil for our doing good to them, when we can't seem to get ahead at work even though we may be the hardest working employees, or when we have to bear the brunt of other people's tragedies without consciously provoking them.

It's also important to understand that this spirit's vicious activity doesn't occur in a vacuum or as an isolated, random event. Instead, these things happen as a result of spiritual doors that we, or our ancestors, have opened, and they willcontinue to happen as a long chain of tragedies, opposition and negative events which seem to have no end in sight.

> Attackers gathered against me without ceasing.
> Like the ungodly, they maliciously mocked me,
> they gnashed their teeth at me. (Psalms 35:15-16 NIV)

King David describes this attack as incessant, concentrated, ruthless and savage. This is exactly how the spirit of injustice operates in our lives, but only when it can find a space to slither itself into. It doesn't matter if this malignant spirit is operating in a person, a family, a nation or a ministry, the results are always just as tragic and catastrophic.

They can also be the result of one particular cycle of tragic events that just repeats itself time and time again in your personal life or family. For example, a sequence of abandonments; families whose members have gone through the painful experience of being abandoned or betrayed by the people they put their trust in. Families that have been victims of a recurring cycles of tragic death, false testimony, legal battles, job loss, ministerial stagnancy, and more, in a way that cannot be explained in the natural.

Many times, people that are under attack by these evil spirits, reach a point where they become saturated with emotional, physical and spiritual exhaustion, because they have spent all their energy trying to change the unjust circumstances which have flooded their surroundings.

This loss of energy can be caused by the staggering effort used defending their integrity against all the false accusations, and then trying to cope with all the emotional damage these horrible spirits have caused in their lives. This energy lossmay also be due to the huge effort they make in ardently working to advance their lives, or perhaps even investing so much time in prayer, yet still feeling as though they're all alone against the world.

We then reach the point of total exhaustion and despair, we can often feel like King David did when he cried out, "Lord, how long will you look on? Rescue my life from their savages, my precious life from these lions" (Psalms 53:17 NIV). This lament King David made to God shows us just how desperate he felt while under the incessant attack of the spirit of injustice.

As I have mentioned before, this evil spirit can attack us so much that we begin to lose faith in God's love and the protection He has for us.

Where Is God?

We can now confirm that people who have been under attack like this tend to lose their faith. This is because they can't understand why an almighty and benevolent God would allow such atrocities to happen. Here is where it is vitally important that everyone understands that it is *not God* who is allowing these bad things in our lives. *It is us!* We are the only ones responsible for keeping the doors shut to all those evil spirits, *not God!*

God, in his infinite wisdom, has given us free will to make decisions and choose certain things for ourselves, and he has reserved others for his choosing. Having said this, one of the options God has given us the power to choose from is whether or not we wish to be truly free.

In other words, if God were to intervene in every single aspect of our lives, it would eliminate all our options of deciding, electing or choosing the things we want. This is the essence of free will. Can we even imagine what it would be like if God didn't let us choose who we were going to marry, the clothes we were going to wear, the words we were going to speak, the places we wanted to go, or any of the multitude of decisions that we get to make on a daily basis? This would make God a dictator and not our Father in heaven.

However, this doesn't mean that God doesn't want to be an integral part of our lives or that he doesn't love us. Quite the contrary! God loves us so much, that as a good father always does, he simply wishes to lovingly guide us to our purpose, to help us make good decisions that will dramatically improve the quality of our lives, without forcing himself on us.

> Today I call the heavens and the earth as witnesses against you, that I have set before you life and death, blessings and curses. Now choose life, so that you and your children may live. (Deut. 30:19 NIV)

Allow me to show you what God's position is in regards to the negative things that occur in our lives. Let's use the example of Jacob. You may recall all the hardships that Jacob had to go through in order to receive the visible manifestation of his blessing. Despite the fact that Jacob had already received the patriarchal blessing from his father, he still had to go through some great difficulties in order to reach all the blessings that were spoken over him.

This begs the question of whether it was Isaac's fault (Jacob's father) that Jacob had to go through all those difficulties in order to see the manifestation of his blessing? Definitely not! The one who tricked, lied and manipulated in this situation, was Jacob, not Isaac. (Let's not forget that Isaac was blind.

That's why Jacob was able to trick him.) Again, all the difficult consequences suffered by Jacob were directly related to his own acts of trickery and no one else's. These actions opened the door to the spirit of injustice, and gave it a foothold in his life. This is why Jacob had to work so hard in order to receive his blessings.

This same principle applies to all of us when we open any door to an evil spirit and allow it to operate in our lives. I want to be very clear in the fact that we can open a spiritual door in our lives to this evil spirit without even knowing it.Let's also remember that this silent enemy attacks us by blocking our blessings, and is a phenomenal creator of chaos for our surrounding territory. This doesn't happen because God is doing it, but because we have allowed it into our lives, often in an unconscious way.

However, this doesn't mean that we no longer carry our blessing. That blessing already belongs to us.

RE-ACTIVATING GOD'S BLESSING IN OUR LIVES

> Praise be to the God and Father of our Lord Jesus Christ, who has blessed us in the heavenly realms with every spiritual blessing in Christ. (Eph. 1:3 NIV)

What is actually happening is that the physical manifestations of our blessings are being blocked by actively disobeying the rules and regulations of the Kingdom of God, and allowing evil spirits to enter our lives. Since we are the only ones responsible for allowing evil spirits to access our lives, only we can rebuke it, reject it and remove it from our lives in the name of Jesus. By doing this, we are once again activating God's blessing that is already within us.

There is no other way to activate God's blessings in our lives than by being obedient to him. When we are obedient to

God and his Word, the forces of evil are automatically bound and therefore cannot exercise any authority over us. In the same way that we can open the spiritual door of our lives to evil spirits through sin, we can also open the spiritual door of our lives to the kingdom of God and his blessings by being obedient and following his Word.

In order for this to happen, we must live our lives as true children of light, which is contrary to the dark and unjust operations of the kingdom of darkness. Let's take a closer look at God's Word to see what rules he expects us to follow ashis children.

> ...To be made new in the attitude of your minds; and to put on the new self, created to be like God in true righteousness and holiness. Therefore, each of you must put off falsehood and speak truthfully to his neighbor, for we are all members of one body. Do not let the sun go down while you are still angry and do not give the devil a foothold. He who has been stealing must steal no longer, but must work, doing something useful with his own hands, that he may have something to share with those in need. Do not let any unwholesome talk come out of your mouths, but only what is helpful for building others up according to their needs. And do not grieve the Holy Spirit of God. Get rid of all bitterness, rage and anger, brawling and slander, along with every form of malice. Be kind and compassionate to one another, forgiving each other, just as in Christ God forgave you. Be imitators of God ... and live a life of love, just as Christ loved us and gave himself up for us as a fragrant offering and sacrifice to God. But among you there must not be even a hint of sexual immorality, or of any

> kind of impunity, or of greed, because these are improper for God's holy people. For you were once darkness, but now you are light in the Lord. Live as children of light (for the fruit of the light consists in all goodness, righteousness and truth). Have nothing to do with the fruitless deeds of darkness, but rather expose them. For it is shameful even to mention what the disobedient do in secret. (Eph. 4:24-5:12 NIV)

These are the principles of justice that God wants His people to follow if it is truly their desire to walk in obedience, and with that obedience comes the blessing. In other words, it is virtually impossible to receive the promise ofGod's blessing if we are not willing to behave at the levels of our identity in Christ.

> For of this you can be sure; No immoral, impure or greedy person -- such a man is an idolater -- has any inheritance in the kingdom of Christ and of God. (Eph. 5:5 NIV)

God's blessing is a gift that was given to all of us by the sacrifice of Jesus on the cross at Calvary, and we can only access it by being obedient to His Word. Any true inheritance (for example, money or heirlooms willed to family members), can only be received when there is a death. In order to receive our inheritance in Christ, we must first "die in the flesh." We must kill all sin and its desires. When we do this, we can then rightfully claim the inheritance of God's blessing which was given to us by the sacrifice of Jesus on the cross.

The Dominion God Has Given Us

When God created man, one of the most valuable assets He gave us was dominion. This means that we were given the authority to operate over everything in this world.

> You made him a little lower than the angels and crowned him with glory and honor. You made him ruler over the works of your hands; you put everything under his feet; all flocks and herds, and the beasts of the field, the birds of the air, and the fish of the sea, all that swim in paths of the seas. (Psalms 8:5-8 NIV)

God has given us freedom to govern all his creation, which of course includes things like our own bodies, our decisions, our thoughts, and our emotions. However, this also includes authority of dominion over the kingdom of darkness, which was also created by him.

Therefore, if we wish to have God intervene in certain events of our lives, we first have to yield permission to him, which releases God to intervene in both our physical and spiritual dimensions. This is precisely what we do when we pray; we are giving God permission or the "legal authority" to intervene in our situation.

Just like parents can't force their adult children to behave in certain way, something similar happens with our Heavenly Father when it concerns us. In other words, God cannot operate in us or in our lives, unless we give him permission to do so.

Let's look at the following example. As parents who truly love their children, we can't try to control everything about them, or force everything we want on them, especially as they get older. This would make them resentful, and they would be ill-prepared to make their own good decisions in the future. However, once they become adults, it is their right to make bad decisions that will negatively affect their lives. When we see our children making bad decisions, we will always advise and encourage them to make the right ones, and offer support any way we can. It hurts to watch, but once a child becomes an adult, he has the legal right to make choices for his life, good or bad.

The same thing happens with our Father God. He gives us all the key information that will direct us in how to live our lives free of spiritual bindings, full of prosperity, fulfillment and joy. However, it is up to us individually to make the decision whether or not to accept his wise recommendations.

Another example is when children fall into more serious trouble, such as a legal case that ends with a conviction and a prison term. As parents, we want to intervene and change the circumstances of the judge's verdict, but it's not within our power to do so. Because we live in a world with laws, we are subject to obey these laws, and if we break any one of them, there are consequences we must face.

The same circumstances apply when we transgress the established laws of God's spirit world. When we sin against the divine rules and regulations of God's kingdom, we have to face the consequences of our sin, even though God would like to intervene, he can't, because the sin has breached his established law. Remember that we were given the authority over our lives, and only we can undo the works of these slimy spirits. We can accomplish this task by activating this authority through our prayers and by asking God for forgiveness through our confessions. Through this process, we are then able to access God's grace and mercy. Now we are ready to receive our righteous deliverance through God's forgiveness of our sins.

How to Be Victorious Over the Spirit of Injustice

So how do we start to make the good decisions for our lives, and break the power of the spirit of injustice? By doing the exact opposite of what it has been telling you to do.

As I have mentioned before, the spirit of injustice is not often confronted by believers because of its extreme subtleness in the way it operates. Common sense tells us that we cannot confront what we don't know is there, so we certainly cannot rebuke something when we aren't even aware it exists.

I have also mentioned that the spirit of injustice hides behind the social and cultural norms of our nations. A good example of this is when we hear people say things like, "I hate to mingle with poor people" (referring to persons who have little or no material resources at all). This evil spirit also hides behind certain racist family customs that are proudly exhibited in expressions like, "My family detests people of color."

This spirit also has a way of slithering into ministries without being detected. For example, church leaders that are placed in positions of power or honor, just for the fact that they have a well known name, or have renown social status. All in all, the spirit of injustice can hide itself within many aspects of everyday human conduct and so many different social, cultural and family parameters that we could write a whole other book on just that.

The good news is that God has given us the Holy Spirit! He allows us to discover and expose this malignant spirit, which finds its way into the body of Christ and the fabric of our society. However, knowing about the existence of this evil spirit and its tricks doesn't mean much if we don't have the weapons necessary to properly fight against it and be free from it in the name of Jesus.

For this task we were given two powerful spiritual weapons by our Lord Jesus Christ. The first is the weapon of prayer. The second is the weapon of endurance. Throughout the New

Testament, we see Jesus tell His disciples over and over again the following words: "Watch and pray so that you may not fall into temptation." (Matt. 26:41 NIV)

The spirit of injustice, as in the case of all malignant spirits, infiltrates and influences our lives through various temptations. However, in the particular case of the spirit of injustice, the methods it uses to tempt us are virtually undetectable. This is precisely why we need to know how to walk in the Spirit.

To accomplish this, we must try and be in prayer as continually as possible, so that we can be warned by the Holy Spirit when we are in danger of being influenced by this slimy spirit.

The second strategy we can use against this evil spirit, is to use endurance in your fight against it, so you ultimately outlast it. This is what Jesus meant when he said to his disciples, "Submit yourselves, then, to God. Resist the devil, and he will flee from you" (James 4:7 NIV). In this case, "resist" means to endure or outlast the attacks and the provocations of the enemy. In other words, God tells us to reject the persuasions of the enemy, no matter how insignificant the temptations might seem. One very effective way to resist something or someone, is to do the exact opposite of what they are instructing us to do.

As humble servants of our Lord and Savior Jesus, and as children that carry his light, we must first acknowledge, discern and evaluate the "value scales" of the society we live in, and the behaviors within our own family, our church and even ourselves, and see if we are all working within the parameters of what God and his kingdom wants us to be in.

We need to make sure that the "justice" we are practicing, as well as the justice that surrounds us, reflects those parameters that rule God's kingdom. We begin of course, by making a truthful evaluation of our own set of standards andguidelines. We need to make sure that we are in step with the way we are behaving and being good stewards of God's kingdom and His justice; not a cheap replica of the unjust parameters that are running rampant in our society.

If our mission is to be the "voice box" of God's good news, and the liberating message of Jesus Christ for social equality, then we're on the right track. What we can't allow to occur, is to try and voice words and attitudes just because it pleases the majority. Our real challenge, if we want to overcome the sneaky spirit of injustice and take its authority away from our lives, is to take a stand that is opposite to what that evil spirit is ministering, or that of the parameters it isrepresenting.

To accomplish this task, we must first renew our own perspective and understanding of our habits, behaviors and attitudes. We can then adopt the righteous culture of God's kingdom.

> Do not conform any longer to the pattern of this world, but be transformed by the renewing of your mind. Then you will be able to test and approve what God's will is-- his good, pleasing and perfect will. (Rom. 12:2 NIV)

To begin this process, it is absolutely key that we renew our minds to the levels of our new identity in Christ! Here's how: if you want to succeed in removing the spirit of injustice from your life, you must spend time in God's presence so you can be filled with the Holy Spirit. When we are filled with the Holy Spirit, there's no room left for any other spirit to infiltrate us.

When we are in the Spirit of our Lord, we also receive the ability to discern what comes from the kingdom of light and what doesn't.

> But when he, the Spirit of truth, comes, he will guide you into all truth. (John 16:13 NIV)

So it doesn't matter how sneaky or slick the spirit of injustice tries to be, the Holy Spirit will always unmask it and flush it out into his light.

It is also through prayer that God empowers us to resist and restrain ourselves from the sinful temptations of the spirit of injustice. Having the ability to resist temptations doesn't come just from having a peaceful and sedentary Christianlifestyle. It actually comes through a sustained lifestyle of spiritual exercise. Just like we need to maintain a consistent routine of exercise in order to stay healthy and develop muscle strength in our bodies, we consistently need to train our spirit through prayer and through God's Word in order to resist the attacks and temptations of the enemy.

It is for precisely this reason that God asks us to pray without ceasing, so we can develop our "spiritual muscles" and so we don't fall victim to the constant lies of the enemy. To resist also means that we must stand firm against the attacks of the enemy. It is just as important to stand firm in the Word of the Lord, if in fact we wish to be victorious over all the temptations that the enemy throws at us.

Once we are well-founded in God's Word, all we have to do to get rid of the malignant influences and temptations, is to reject and rebuke them in the name of Jesus Christ! God wants us to be free of all these malignant spirits, but in order to accomplish this task, we need to be proactive with all the spiritual weapons that God's kingdom has placed at our disposal.

CHAPTER 7

I have mentioned before that only we have the power to rebuke and cancel all the evil spirits from our lives. This task can be accomplished by praying the prayer of renouncement below (more details about this type of prayer can be found in my first book, *Clash Between Two Kingdoms*).

We define renouncement as terminating an alliance, breaking ties of unity, and disassociating yourself with someone or something, The prayer of renouncement has several steps to follow built right in.

First and foremost, we begin with the prayer of confession. This consists of taking responsibility before God for sins we have committed, for generational sins committed by our ancestors, or even for sins committed by our nation.

...The Lord, the Lord, the compassionate and gracious God, slow to anger, abounding in love and faithfulness, maintaining love to thousands, and forgiving wickedness, rebellion and sin. Yet he does not leave the guilty unpunished; he punishes the children and their children for the sin of the parents to the third and fourth generation. (Exod. 34:6-7 NIV)

Secondly, we have the prayer of asking for forgiveness. This is where we ask God to forgive us for our sins, the sins of our ancestors, and those of our nation. Next, we enter the third phase, where we pray the prayer of renouncement. This is where we can apply the true meaning of the the word "renouncement" and disassociate ourselves from, and sever alliances with, all those sins and the evil spirits that are associated with them.

Now we can enter into the fourth phase of this process, which really becomes the most intense section of the prayer. This is where we begin to cast out all these malignant spirits from our lives, and the lives of our descendants, in Jesus name!

The fifth and final step is when we decree against these malignant spirits by declaring them totally null in our lives in the name of Jesus. And we will also take his right to return or to be transferred to our loved ones, in Jesus name!

PRAYER OF RENOUNCEMENT OF THE SPIRIT OF INJUSTICE

1. I ask that you forgive all acts of injustice committed by me and by my ancestors. This includes my parents, my grandparents, my great-grandparents and by any other people of authority over my life. (If you happen to know of any specific sins committed by your ancestors or family members, then mention each one by name and ask God to forgive them.)
2. I ask that you forgive me for every act of injustice I have committed, knowingly or unknowingly, from the day I was born to the present day. (Make sure you mention every one of them very specifically as far as you can remember. Then ask God to forgive each one of them.)
3. I ask, Lord, that you forgive me for every unjust act I have committed, which has resulted in someone being ruined, hurt, wounded, or somehow badly affected by my awful acts. (If it is at all possible, try to contact the people you've wronged and ask them to forgive you.)
4. I now forgive every person who has treated me unjustly, including those who have done physical or verbal damage to me, sexually assaulted me, abused me as a child, committed spousal abuse against me, betrayed me, declared false testimony against me, raped me,

manipulated me, lied to me, tricked me, placed me under forced prostitution, trafficked or exploited me, unjustly dismissed me from work, persistently stalked me, practiced labor exploitations over meor abused their power or authority over me. (If you have suffered any one of these circumstances, make sure to mention the specifics of each situation, as well as the names of the people involved. Then forgive them.) I forgive them and I free them from any more personal judgment. I ask that the Holy Spirit visit them and bring them salvation, peace, deliverance and blessings, in the name of Jesus Christ!

5. I renounce all sentiments of hatred, vengeance, unforgiveness, roots of bitterness, a hardened heart, rejection of everyone, and doubtful and disbelieving mentality that have been operating over my life as a result of all these abuses. I now totally reject them. I bind their operation and influence over my life, and I cancel their rights to operate over me, in Jesus name!

6. I completely renounce all spirits of injustice that have accessed my life through the sins of my ancestors or by unjust acts committed by them. I rebuke them and will not ever accept them back into my life, in the name of Jesus Christ!

7. I renounce all evil spirits of injustice that have accessed my life simply because I live in a nation where this spirit exercises its dominion. I rebuke and reject it from my life, as well as that of my descendants. I cancel its influence over my will, my desires, my preferences, my attitude, my thoughts and my behavior. I cast it out of my life forever, in the name of Jesus!

8. I renounce all practice in my life associated with the spirits of injustice that have been operating my life through unjust decisions I have made in the past, knowingly or unknowingly, through negative words

pronounced by me, through cursed words, through judgmental words, by falsely accusing my neighbors and by pointing out everyone else's wrongdoings. I cancel out all these words and I remove the power of spirit of injustice to ever exercise its influence over my life again, in the name of Jesus!

9. I cancel all assignments of the spirit of injustice from my life through santeria, witchcraft, sorcery, demonic curses, satanic incantations and blood pacts. I now declare them powerless and inoperable in my life, in the name of Jesus!

10. I bind the operation of the spirit of injustice over my marriage, over my children, my work, my finances, and over all my personal relationships. I bind all influences regarding my reputation, my health, my projects, my faith and over all channels of prosperity related to my life, in Jesus name!

11. I sever all roots of the spirit of injustice that oppose me in reaching my God-given destiny. I declare that all the sinful roots of this evil spirit that have been active in my life are now dried up, in Jesus name!

12. I now cancel all assignments of this scummy spirit of injustice that have been sent to attack my name and my that of my family members, through unjust cycles of actions, such as recurring divorces, cycles of abandonment, cycles of sexual, physical and emotional abuse, cycles of poverty, cycles of tragedy, cycles of early death of people close to me, cycles of suicide, cycles of depression, constant job loss and constant cycles of failure. (Mention any other cycles that might be operating in your life, or that of your family.) I now break all these cycles in the name of Jesus Christ, and I subject all the evil spirits that are associated with these slimy spirits to be inoperable in my life and in the lives

of my descendants, in the name, and by the blood, of Jesus Christ!

13. I suppress all authority of this evil spirit of injustice which is exerting influence over the culture of my nation, over my family, over my church, over my concepts and perceptions, and over my ideas and parameters. Today, I take authority over this malignant spirit, and I bind its abilities to control my life. I also bind any and all influences it might have over the lives of my family, my culture, my church and my nation, in the mighty name of Jesus!

14. I cast out all these evil spirits from my life and I shut all doors that might have been opened by this evil spirit in my life and in all the lives of my descendants, permanently and forever, in Jesus name!

15. I now establish in my life all the just principles that govern the kingdom of light and I decree that they are established permanently in my life, the lives of my family, my projects and my nation, in the name of Jesus!

DECREE OF DELIVERANCE FROM THE SPIRIT OF INJUSTICE

I declare that I am a child of God, and as a child of His, I am a co-heir with Christ of all his promises. Therefore, I refuse to accept any device or lies from the enemy directed to my mind. I cancel all words that have been spoken over my life that are opposite to the kingdom of light that I belong to.

I accept the redeeming power of the blood of Jesus Christ, which cleanses me from all my sins.

I declare that all doors that have been opened in my life to the spirit of injustice by generational curses, personal sins I have committed, evil territorial influences or malignant assignments are now shut completely, in the name of Jesus!

I bind the power of the spirit of injustice so he can no longer exercise authority over my life, my thoughts, my words or my faith. I now relinquish all authority to the Holy Spirit to govern these areas of my life. I declare that from now on, only the Holy Spirit will have the absolute right to direct my life, according to the parameters of justice which operate in God's kingdom.

I shut the doors of my life against all voices that come from the kingdom of darkness, and which have intended to work against me through social rules and norms, cultural falsehoods, shameful family behaviors, excessive piety, or that intend to establish unjust behaviors in me that do not conform to the written Word of God. I reject and rebuke them all, in Jesus name! I declare that any negative authority that the spirit of injustice might have over my life has now been invalidated forever, in the name of Jesus!

I speak blessings over my life, and I now order the spirit of injustice to return sevenfold everything that it has stolen from my spiritual life, my family life, my financial life and my social life, in the name of Jesus!

I declare null and void all curses which I have proclaimed through false testimony, negative criticism, judgmental behavior and taking unfair advantage of people that were actually trying to help me. I activate the culture of God's kingdom to take over my mind, my words, my attitude and my behavior, to allow me to better appreciate others according to God's divine system, and not those of terrestrial systems.

I confess that I'm free from all oppression exercised by the spirit of injustice that has an impact over my character through a hardened heart, indifference, disloyalty, sudden bursts of temper, arrogance, hypocrisy, extreme sensitivity, or through being double-minded.

I declare that I am free from every malignant influence which has tried to take over my emotions through roots of bitterness, hatred, resentment, rejection, depression, fear, untrustworthiness, desires of vengeance or low self-esteem. I establish that it no longer has a binding hold over my life, and

I now give the Holy Spirit complete authority to operate in all these aspects of my life, in the name of Jesus Christ!

I declare that my character is governed by God's Spirit and that his fruits, which are love, peace, patience, goodness, joy, kindness, faithfulness, forbearance, gentleness, self-control, are all established over my life, in the mighty name of Jesus Christ!

I declare and decree that I am free from all evil cycles of injustice which have been operating in my life through constant job loss; legal persecution; cycles of divorce; betrayal; physical, sexual and emotional abuse, cycles of failure, abandonment or infidelity. They have no room in my life or that of my descendants. I cast them out now, in the name of Jesus!

Today, I am establishing a new cycle of divine justice over my life that will be manifested through integrity, emotional stability, inner peace, prosperity in my ministry, abundance in my finances, a stable marriage and through the visible manifestation of all the blessings that God has destined for me! I declare and decree that all of God's promises for my life that have been detained by the spirit of injustice, are now released, in the name of Jesus Christ!

I now declare a whole new cycle of very good news over my life, and a complete restoration of all affected areas that the evil spirit of injustice has attacked. I speak peace over my territory and I establish that all unjust cycles of sudden death, poverty, catastrophe, rape, human violation, human trafficking or forced prostitution, is now detained, in the name of Jesus!

I now declare that the kingdom of God and his government of justice are established over my nation. I declare that my nation is showered with all the just parameters, riches and blessings that come from the kingdom of light. I declare that all devices of the enemy against my nation are completely invalidated by the blood of Jesus!

I declare and decree that all evil voices that have been raised up against my life, family and nation are now blocked, in the name of Jesus. I now cut ties with every spiritual pact or alliance made with the spirit of injustice. I now declare it null and void in my life, the lives of my descendants and over my nation, in the name of Jesus!

I now open my spiritual ears to receive the guidance of the Holy Spirit, which will lead me to all truth and righteousness. I now make a divine alliance with the kingdom of light, so I can operate on earth in the same dimension that my Father operates in heaven. All these things I declare and decree in the mighty name of Jesus Christ. Amen!

Prayer is the indispensable tool that we need in order to cast out and sever the influences of any evil spirits, including the spirit of injustice. The following journey of prayer will also be accompanied by fasting. When we combine the additional act of fasting with prayer, we are uniting two very powerful spiritual weapons to counterattack the evil influences of these malignant spirits and all other spirits that are associated with it.

The main reason Jesus recommended fasting to His disciples was because there were intensities of demonic levels that could only be defeated by joining the two spiritual weapons of prayer and fasting (Matt. 17:21).

Aside from being a powerful spiritual weapon, fasting also serves as a method to strengthen our own faith and spiritual life. This strengthening of our faith allows us to stand firmly against the whispers and workings of the enemy.

In the case of the spirit of injustice, we find that it occupies a very high rank in the evil kingdom of darkness. This is due to its stealthy ability to affect anyone anywhere, its wide range of attack patterns, its ability to leave a huge path of chaos and destruction, and how it can work in association with such a wide variety of other evil spirits.

Day By Day Prayer Guide.

This journey of deliverance will consist of three days of prayer and fasting. The fasting should last no less than seven hours. In other words, if you start your fast at about 6:00 a.m., you should last at least until 1:00 p.m. that same day. However you can extend your fasting period for longer if you wish. As you abstain from food during this time, please remember to stay safely hydrated, and drink water or other liquids.

This journey may also be used as a group event on the congregational level, or you can simply use it as an individual project. This three day journey of prayer and fasting will follow the exact framework of the "prayer of renunciation of the spirit of injustice," which we went over in the previous several pages.

When you are declaring each renouncement, and making your confessions to the Lord, try and be as specific as possible, and include as many details as you can. Don't forget that God loves truthfulness and honesty when we are confessing before Him. Also, don't forget to ask the Holy Spirit to assist you in your memory lapses.

It is very important to begin these journeys with a time of praise and worship. This opens the door to the Holy Spirit so he can provide the direction of each prayer session.

Enter his gates with thanksgiving and his courts with praise; give thanks to him and praise his name. (Psalms 100:4 NIV)

At the end of your three day journey, you may remember someone that you forgot to mention in your prayer time before. You can still forgive them and mention their name in an audible voice. For example, you can simply say, "I forgive you, I let you go, and I take away my judgements against you, in the name of Jesus!" It is also very important to speak in an audible voice at all times when you are participating in each session of these prayers of renunciation. Remember, only God can hear silent thoughts and prayers, and knows what is in your mind. Demons can only hear and obey audible commands.

If you would like to know more on the different types of prayers, you can learn much more about them in my first book, *Clash Between Two Kingdoms*.

When beginning each session of praise and worship, it's important to do this either kneeling in surrender or laying face down on the floor. This is to show absolute reverence to our Lord and Creator. However, when we get ready to make our declarations of renouncement, this we must do standing up or sitting upright in a chair. We take this stance because of the powerful nature needed to implement this particular weapon of spiritual warfare. Don't forget that you must have water or other liquids handy so you can stay hydrated during these prayer sessions.

FIRST DAY OF PRAYER

The first day of our prayer journey consists of confessing our sins and asking for God's forgiveness. This means that we will be asking God to forgive all our sins as we confess each one of them. We will also forgive those who have done us wrong in one way or another and we accomplish this by praying the prayer of renouncement found in the previous pages. In other words, our first day will include paragraphs one through five of the prayer of renouncement.

If we confess our sins, he is faithful and just and will forgive us our sins and purify us from all unrighteousness. (1 John 1:9 NIV)

The passage of scripture that we will be reading from is Psalms 51. At the end of the day's journey, we will conclude our prayer day by reading and declaring the decree of deliverance from the spirit of injustice out loud.

SECOND DAY OF PRAYER

On this day, we will once again enter into God's presence by worshipping and surrendering ourselves to him. Then we will begin a systematic renouncement of all the ancestral sins that have been operating in our family, as well as all spirits of injustice that operate in our territory and that have been activated by our unjust behavior and unsubstantiated judgement against others.

We will also be renouncing the evil spirits of injustice that were activated in our lives through practices of the occult. In other words, we will be declaring paragraphs six through nine of the prayer of renouncement in an audible voice.

The bible reading for this second day of prayer can be found in Psalms 35. Finally, as we'll do at the end of each prayer day, we will conclude it by declaring the decree of deliverance from the spirit of injustice out loud.

THIRD DAY OF PRAYER

On this third and final day of our prayer journey, we will once again approach the presence of the Lord through our praise and surrender to him. After we praise God, and confess our sins of the day to him, we can begin to declare paragraphs ten through thirteen of the prayer of renouncement out loud.

We will be renouncing all evil spirits of injustice that have been exercising influence over our lives, our marriage, our faith, our health, our reputation and our ministry. We will next renounce and cancel all cycles of injustice that have slithered into our lives via the spirit of injustice by declaring paragraph fourteen in an audible voice.

We will then exercise authority over this malignant spirit and declare it powerless over our culture, our family, our church, our society and our nation by proclaiming paragraph fifteen in the prayer of renouncement aloud.

At this point, we will systematically begin to close all the doors that have been opened in our lives to those evil spirits. We will then activate the principles of justice that govern God's kingdom, and establish them in our lives, in Jesus' name! The bible reading for this third day is Psalms 9.

Once you have finished your three day prayer journey, try and maintain your own spirit with an attitude of receiving all the new and good things that God has destined for your life. Get ready to experience the freedom and abundant life that God has called you to live in.

So if the Son sets you free, you will be free indeed. (John 8:36 NIV)

Why We Should Operate In Truth And Justice

> But seek first His kingdom and His righteousness,
> and all these things will be given to you as well.
> (Matt. 6:33 NIV)

At the beginning of this book, we learned that one of the principal reasons Jesus came to earth was to establish his kingdom of justice over that of the kingdom of darkness, which seemed to have established a stronghold over the terrestrial governments.

The fundamental principle of God's kingdom is the issue of justice. This is precisely why, as God's children and good stewards of his earth, it is indispensable to God that we also try to operate in justice. In Matthew 6:33, Jesus tells his disciples to seek first the kingdom of God and his righteousness if they wish to obtain the life of fulfillment that He has designed for them, and live under open heavens.

In other words, everything we could wish for or dream about, everything our hearts desire and everything that God wants to deliver to us, depends on us being able to operate in justice. So if we truly wish to receive all our blessings, we must first be diligent and search for God's kingdom and his righteousness.

This verse also sheds some light on why it is that we can pray and yet not seem to receive any answers to those prayers.

Often it's because we are conducting ourselves unjustly. This is why it is imperative for us to seek first God's kingdom and his justice before we can receive the answers to our prayers. Operating in unjust behavior is what actually impedes God from hearing our prayers and granting our requests.

> But your iniquities have separated you from your God; your sins have hidden his face from you, so that he will not hear. For your hands are stained with blood, your fingers with guilt. Your lips have spoken lies, and your tongue mutters wicked things. No one calls for justice; no one pleads his case with integrity. They rely on empty arguments and speak lies; they conceive trouble and give birth to evil. (Isa. 59:2-4 NIV)

As we read this passage, we can understand that the word "iniquity" also means injustice, something distorted. In verse three of the same chapter, we are given a rather long list of these unjust practices that God rejects, such as acts of bloodshed, lies, evil works, and unfair judgements. All these bad behaviors are directly linked to the spirit of injustice and form an essential part of the manner in which it operates.

It is also very clear that these forms of bad behavior result in a direct separation of God from those who decide to go down the path of iniquity. The Bible goes much further in letting us know that when we make the decision to operate in the spirit of injustice, God not only separates himself from us, but also hides his face so he doesn't hear us.

This is a partial explanation as to why our prayers sometimes feel blocked, or why a nation may seem to have been forgotten by God, or that whole families, churches and ministries are withering away. It is your typical cause and effect situation. According to Isaiah 59, If we walk the path of iniquity, God will hide his face so he can't listen to our prayers. It's that simple.

73

When I was writing this book, it was revealed to me that the conflicts which Israel has been suffering for so many centuries, stem from a long history of iniquities committed by God's people of Israel. The Bible is very clear in identifying Israel as God's chosen people, and that those who choose to bless Israel will themselves be blessed. Conversely, those who choose to condemn Israel, shall be condemned.

I found myself in a conundrum because the question arose in my mind that If God chose Israel to be his chosen people, why is it that we have seen constant conflicts that have caused them so much death and destruction throughout its history? We can even see the horrific conflicts continue today with the radical terrorist group Hamas, who has sworn to annihilate all of Israel. We also have Iran developing nuclear weapons to wipe Israel off the world map. I had to ask myselfwhy God doesn't just come out and prevent these potential threats and massacres from happening to his chosen people?

When the Holy Spirit lead me to Isaiah 59 and exposed the revelation of Israel's situation of constant persecution, I was truly amazed how clear he made it to me! It allowed me to see all the doors that the people of Israel had opened because of the many recurring sins they committed throughout their history. Through their many sins, the people of Israel had opened the door to the spirit of injustice to operate over their nation, and consequently over their lives.

We see the destructive nature of this evil spirit operating in the nation of Israel through its many wars, conflicts, deaths of innocent people, betrayals, uprisings and the multitude of other nations that hate this nation, because they too are under the influence of this spirit. As we read all of Isaiah 59, it is evident that we find out why it is that God separated Himself from His chosen people.

> Their feet rush into sin; they are swift to shed
> innocent blood. Their thoughts are evil thoughts;

ruin and destruction mark their ways. The way
of peace they do not know; there is no justice in
their paths. They have turned them into crooked
roads; no one who walks in them will know
peace. (Isa. 59:7-8 NIV)

All these doors, that have been opened by the people of
Israel, under the influence of this evil spirit of injustice, have
created a division between God and his chosen people, which
impedes him from intervening in their lives. It's not that God
isn't aware of, or is indifferent to, the difficulties of his chosen
nation, it's the fact that they have allowed the infiltration of
theses sneaky evil spirits into their lives, thus inhibiting God's
divine assistance to reach them.

We all growl like bears; we moan mournfully
like doves. We look for justice, but we find none;
for deliverance, but it is far away. For our offenses
are many in our sight, and our sins testify
against us. Our offenses are ever with us, and
we acknowledge our iniquities: rebellion and
treachery against the Lord, turning our backs on
our God, inciting oppression and revolt, uttering
lies our hearts have conceived. So justice is driven
back, and righteousness stands at a distance;
truth has stumbled in the streets, honesty cannot
enter. Truth is nowhere to be found, and whoever
shuns evil, becomes a prey. The Lord looked and
was displeased that there was no justice. (Isa.
59:11-15 NIV)

These very revealing words from our Lord sum up the
terrible effects that these evil spirits of injustice have upon our
lives, as well as in our nation, when we allow them to enter and

set up operations. This is precisely what has happened with the nation of Israel, even though they are still God's chosen people.

We even see that the apostle Paul had similar concerns over the nation of Israel when he said, "Brothers, my heart's desire and prayer to God for the Israelites is that they may be saved. For I can testify about them that they are zealous for God, but their zeal is not based on knowledge. Since they did not know the righteousness that comes from God and sought to establish their own, they did not submit to God's righteousness" (Rom. 10:1-3 NIV).

We clearly see how the people of Israel were being directed by their own sense of righteousness and not that of God's kingdom. It is because of this conscious or unconscious disobedience in not seeking God's righteousness that we have seen the history of constant wars, violent confrontations and the loss of many innocent lives being activated over this nation. The spirit of injustice has brought and caused cycles of persecution, cycles of constant attack and a chain of warring conflicts to the nation of Israel with no foreseeable end in sight.

Even today, Israel's desire to achieve peace is certainly a genuine aspiration, but until it breaks from the previous pacts they've made with the spirit of injustice, which have opened the doors to all these evil and bloody cycles, they will not be able to see peace. Just as the Lord has asked all of us to do, Israel must also retract themselves from all activities of iniquity. Israel must first do this before God can reactivate his pacts of peace toward them.

We must be very cautious to point out that just because a nation or an individual person is under the evil oppression or influence of the spirit of injustice, doesn't mean that God's plan for them are not going to be accomplished.

> Did God reject his people? By no means! I am
> an Israelite myself, a descendant of Abraham,

from the tribe of Benjamin. God did not reject
his people, whom he foreknew. (Rom. 11:1-2 NIV)

When we indulge in elements of sin, it is the automatic
reaction of God to "hide his face" from us, as we see when
Isaiah says, "your iniquities have separated you from your
God; your sins have hidden his face from you, so that he will
not hear" (Isa. 59:2 NIV).

Now we have arrived at the million dollar question. What
were the generational sins committed by the nation of Israel
that opened the doors to the spirit of injustice in the first place?
We can actually find the answer by referring to Isaiah 59:7-
8, where it says, "Their feet rush into sin; they are swift to
shed innocent blood. Their thoughts are evil thoughts; ruin
and destruction mark their ways. The way of peace they do
not know; there is no justice in their paths. They have turned
them into crooked roads; no one who walks in them will know
peace."

All these sinful practices are closely related to the spirit of
injustice and they open the doors to operate within a nation for
generations to come. But despite all these faults, "The Redeemer
will come to Zion, to those in Jacob who repent of their sins,
declares the Lord." (Isaiah 59: 20 NIV).

This is where I need to take a bit of pause, so I can explain
in better detail the importance of this revelation given to me by
the Holy Spirit. This is also where we can see the importance of
getting to know our spiritual family tree and what it can reveal
to us about the sinful inheritance that we carry. I cannot stress
enough that this is the single most important revelation I have
had and it is the main reason for having written this book!

We know that Jacob was the son of Isaac and Rebecca, and
that Jacob is known as being the "Father of Israel." In other
words, the nation of Israel is the direct descendant of Jacob.

You may recall that Jacob's life had been infiltrated by the
spirit of injustice, and we learned the many ways it followed

him throughout his life. We also mentioned how Rebecca aligned herself with Jacob in order to trick Isaac (his father), so Jacob could steal the "blessing of the first born" from his brother, Esau.

It is important that we understand that this first act of trickery was the very act that opened the door to the malignant spirit of injustice, and that what occurred in Jacob's life, and that of all his descendants, originates from this initial act of trickery. These include events like persecution, death, unjust behavior, the tragic early death of his wife Rachel, and the apparent loss of his favorite son, Joseph.

We have made it clear that the spirit of injustice had come via the generation of Jacob's mother, and his uncle Laban. We see a clear generational transfer of this sneaky spirit of injustice as it is transferred to Jacob's sons, when theysell Joseph and then trick their father into believing that Joseph had been devoured by a lion.

By all intents and purposes, Jacob had opened the door to the spirit of injustice and his sons reinforced these cycles of injustice by actively participating in even worse behavior. This consequently opened the door to their following generations. As we continue to study Isaiah 59, we get a bigger picture of what happens when the spirit of injustice is spread from one generation to another.

> For your hands are stained with blood, your fingers with guilt. Your lips have spoken lies, and your tongue mutters wicked things. No one calls for justice; no one pleads his case with integrity. They rely on empty arguments and speak lies; they conceive trouble and give birth to evil. (Isa. 59:3-4 NIV)

It becomes the sum total of all these evil acts that the spirit of injustice is reinforced through an individual, then a family, and then through a nation, that allows it to grow and strengthen its grip.

I can only imagine that the present generation of Israelis are totally unaware of the origins of the many continuous attacks from all sides, that they've had to experience. They cannot understand why it is that there is so much animosity and hatred against them, even from nations with which they have no quarrel.

You might even find the Israeli people asking themselves the question, "Why hasn't the bloodshed left our nation?" Or maybe "Why is it that we keep seeking peace and yet we are still attacked without provocation?" The answer lies in the generational pacts of iniquities, activated so many years ago by their father, Jacob!

The nation of Israel needs to heed God's call in Isaiah 59:20, where he cries out, "The Redeemer will come to Zion, to those in Jacob, who repent of their sins." We recognize that the Redeemer has already come: Jesus Christ.Unfortunately, to this date, Israel has not accepted Jesus as the Messiah or as the Son of God. This denial only reinforces all the evil bindings, iniquities and injustices that operate within them, through the influence of the spirit of injustice.

By not accepting these elements of biblical history, the people of Israel have essentially denied themselves the benefits of the redeeming power of the blood of Jesus Christ. So it's up to the people of Israel to free and heal their land from the generational grip of the spirit of injustice that it has had over it for so many centuries past.

By doing so, it will reactivate the original pact that God made with his chosen people of Israel. Israel needs to humble themselves before God, make their confession of sins and renounce them all, in the name of Jesus Christ! Finally, they need to return their hearts to the Lord and align their actions and behaviors to God's will. They also need to accept the biblical fact that the Messiah did come, his name is Jesus Christ and that he is the Son of God!

> "As for me, this is my covenant with them," says the Lord, "My Spirit, who is on you, and my words that I have put in your mouth will not depart from your mouth, or the mouths of your children, or from the mouths of theirdescendants from this time on and forever," says the Lord. (Isa. 59:21 NIV).

As this passage clearly states, God still maintains his original position with regard to his chosen people of Israel. Even though their sins have invalidated the pacts of peace God has made with Israel, God is still waiting for them to turn away from their crooked paths, so he can make new pacts with them.

God loves his people of Israel so much that he has asked all of us to pray for them continually. God has gone as far as to promise us blessings if we bless Israel, and curse those who dare to curse Israel. It is vital for all believers to pray for deliverance and peace for the nation of Israel. Let's not forget the promise that God made to Abraham (the father of Isaac and grandfather of Jacob), that through him all nations would be blessed, and that God's promises are permanent and unequivocal.

For God's gifts and his call are irrevocable. (Rom. 11:29 NIV)

This all means that if we wish to see the physical manifestation of God's blessing over our own nation, we simply need to pray for Israel. When Israel is victorious, then the totality of the body of Christ is also victorious!

> And so all of Israel will be saved, as it is written: 'The deliverer will come from Zion; he will take godlessness away from Jacob. And this is my

covenant with them when I take away their sins.
(Rom. 11:26-27 NIV)

However, it is still very curious to me to see people participating in the unjust practices that we have just mentioned, and still believe that God is indifferent to those practices. Allow me to state a resounding "NO!" to this mistaken thought process. God hates all sin with equal displeasure! Even when we indulge in what we might think are "small sins," God sees them the same way. God will not listen to to our prayers and petitions, because all sin blocks his listening to us.

It all boils down to one basic decision that we must face in our lives: do we want to serve the kingdom of God and seek his righteousness, or do we want to be part of the kingdom of darkness and all of its injustice? If your answer is to seek and serve God and his righteousness, then you have chosen to live under open heavens, and your actions and decisions should reflect the parameters that operate within the kingdom of light.

When we decide to operate within righteousness, God's Word tells us that the heavens will be opened to us. How does this occur? When we practice justice, we are being obedient to the Word of God, and this obedience is what opens the heavens.

> If you fully obey the Lord your God and carefully follow all his commands I give you today, the Lord your God will set you high above all the nations on the earth. All these blessings will come upon you and accompany you if you obey the Lord your God. (Deut. 28:1-2 NIV)

> The Lord will open the heavens, the storehouse of his bounty, to send rain on your land in season and to bless all the work of your hands. You will

lend to many nations but will borrow from none.
(Deut. 28:12 NIV)

Simply put, all we must do to live under open heavens is be obedient to God and His Word. If we choose to be disobedient, then we are actively opening the doors of our lives to all sorts of curses.

> However, if you do not obey the Lord your God and do not carefully follow all his commands and decrees I am giving you today, all these curses will come upon you and overtake you. (Deut. 28:15 NIV)

To willfully operate in righteousness means you are acting in obedience. Justice is a major component of the rules, regulations and principles that rule the kingdom of God, and as his servants, we are expected to obey them all. When we do violate any one of these rules, we are automatically breaking his divine commandments and this is what we identify as "sin" (1 John 3:4).

Throughout biblical history, God has always been very clear about the rules and regulations that run his kingdom. This clarity gives us a chance to fulfill these rules, so we can enjoy all the benefits of his blessings. However, temptation will always be our adversary, and the devil will always try to persuade us to disobey God's rules. Let's not forget that the devil does this to purposely throw us off track, and force us into its web of chaos and curses, preventing us from reaching God's promises.

We can go all the way back to when God decided to free his people from slavery in Egypt. Ever since then, God has made sure to instruct the Israelites on the rules that govern his just kingdom. God knew that his chosen people also had firsthand knowledge of the unjust laws that the Egyptians had been imposing on them for the past 400 years. So it was urgent that God instruct Israel carefully in how to operate within the parameters of his kingdom of light, and not simply fall back on what they had learned from the Egyptian government.

In Leviticus 17, we see how God began to teach the nation of Israel the sanctity and justice of his heavenly government and how it functions.

THE LAWS OF HEALING AND RIGHTEOUSNESS.

> You must not do as they do in Egypt, where you used to live, and you must not do as they do in the land of Canaan, where I am bringing you. Do not follow their practices. (Lev. 18:3 NIV)

These new rules and regulations that God had provided for his chosen people were a whole new set of codes - ethical, social and even spiritual - all based on God's just behavior, which he also demands from his people.

It was actually a transformation of their perspective of values and honor toward God himself, as well as a new perspective of respect and love for one another. In other words, God wanted to renew the minds of his chosen ones. God wanted to make sure that they could receive the new identity he had prepared for them. That is to say, God wanted to remove their old Egyptian mentality and transform their minds to become the Chosen People of God.

Let's take a small journey through the book of Leviticus, chapters 18 and 19, and we can itemize these new parameters of righteousness that God wanted to plant into his people:

1. The law of righteousness over adultery.

   "Do not have sexual relations with your neighbor's wife and defile yourself with her" (Lev. 18:20 NIV).

2. The law of righteousness over homosexuality.

   "Do not lie with a man as one lies with a woman; that is detestable" (Lev. 18:22 NIV).

3. The law of righteousness over idolatry.

   "Do not turn to idols or make gods of cast metal for yourselves, I am the Lord your God." (Lev. 19:4 NIV).

   "Do not turn to mediums or seek out spiritists, for you will be defiled by them. I am the Lord your God" (Lev. 19:31 NIV).

4. The law of righteousness against trickery, lying and stealing.

   "Do not steal. Do not deceive one another" (Lev. 19:11 NIV).

5. The law of righteousness against swearing.

   "Do not swear falsely by my name and so profane the name of your God. I am the Lord" (Lev. 19:12 NIV).

6. The law of righteousness against prostitution and human trafficking.

"Do not degrade your daughter by making her a prostitute, or the land will turn to prostitution and be filled with wickedness" (Lev. 19:29 NIV).

7. The law of righteousness against oppression.

   "Do not defraud your neighbor or rob him. Do not hold back the wages of a hired man overnight" (Lev. 19:13 NIV).

8. The law of righteousness against abusers.

   "Do not curse the deaf or put a stumbling block in front of the blind, but fear your God. I am the Lord" (Lev. 19:14 NIV).

9. The law of righteousness against injustice.

   "Do not pervert justice; do not show partiality to the poor or favoritism to the great, but judge your neighbor fairly" (Lev. 19:15 NIV).

   "Do not use dishonest standards when measuring length, weight or quantity. Use honest scales and honest weights, an honest ephah and an honest hin. I am the Lord your God who brought you out of Egypt" (Lev. 19:35-36 NIV).

10. The law of righteousness against gossip.

    "Do not go about spreading slander among your people" (Lev. 19:16 NIV).

11. The law of righteousness against hatred.

"Do not hate your brother in your heart. Rebuke your neighbor frankly so you will not share in his guilt" (Lev. 19:17 NIV).

12. The law of righteousness against murder.

"Do not do anything that endangers your neighbors life" (Lev. 19:16 NIV).

13. The law of righteousness against vengeance and grudges.

"Do not seek revenge or bear a grudge against one of your people, but love your neighbor as yourself. I am the Lord" (Lev. 19:18 NIV).

14. The law of righteousness against the oppression of the foreign-born immigrants.

"The alien living with you must be treated as one of your native-born. Love him as yourself, for you were aliens in Egypt. I am the Lord your God" (Lev. 19:34 NIV).

15. The law of righteousness in favor of respect to the elderly.

"Rise in the presence of the aged, show respect for the elderly and revere your God. I am the Lord." (Leviticus 19: 32 NIV).

16. The law of righteousness in favor of love.

"… But love your neighbor as yourself. I am the Lord" (Lev. 19:18 NIV).

> Keep my requirements and do not follow any of
> the detestable customs that were practiced before
> you came and do not defile yourselves with them.
> I am the Lord your God. (Lev. 18:30 NIV).

It is quite clear that by exposing his people to these new rules and regulations, it was, and continues to be, God's intent to guide them into operating in justice. It is imperative, as ambassadors of God's kingdom here on earth, that we actively operate within the principles of God's rules, now that we have embraced our new identity in Christ.

AMBASSADORS OF GOD'S KINGDOM

> We are therefore Christ's ambassadors, as though
> God were making his appeal through us. We
> implore you on Christ's behalf: Be reconciled to
> God. (2 Cor. 6:20 NIV)

The principal function of an ambassador is to represent their nation or government when traveling to foreign nations. An ambassador does so by faithfully representing their country's customs, culture, laws and principles, in the nations they are visiting.

It is precisely for this reason, that as faithful ambassadors of God's kingdom here on earth, we need to make sure that we emulate a just behavior that aligns itself with the laws and principles that rule the kingdom we are representing. This means that when we fall into unjust practices, we are not being good ambassadors to God's kingdom, but rather we are now participating in the access of evil behavior. This is when we open the spiritual doors of our lives to the spirit of injustice and we start to be influenced, controlled and directed by his evil doing.

Another reason we must always function in righteousness, is because we are the justice of God.

> God made him who had no sin to be sin for us, so
> that in him we might become the righteousness
> of God. (2 Cor. 5:21 NIV)

To be the righteousness of God, I believe, is one of the greatest challenges we face as Christians. To be the righteousness of God implies that our lives, through our daily actions and behavior, must reflect God's righteousness here on earth. We must do this even if it means going against our own wishes.

You may be asking yourself, "How can I accomplish such a task?" Well, I'm so glad you asked. Since we are made of flesh and blood, we must first "die to our flesh." Our "flesh" here refers to the fact that because we are human, we naturally operate in sinful human traits, such as hatred, discrimination, resentment, overzealousness, arrogance, feelings of vengeance and so on. However, if we really want to fulfill our mission to God, in representing his righteousness here on earth, we must first crucify our flesh and its desires.

> Those who belong to Christ Jesus have crucified
> the sinful nature with its passions and desires.
> (Gal. 5:24 NIV)

We do this by purposefully deciding to live our lives within the confines of God's righteousness, even when it goes against our humanity and our desires. Another way we can look at this important component is to think of it in reverse. If we decide *not* to walk in the ways our Lord has taught us, then we would be walking in disobedience, and as a direct consequence, we would be activating curses in our lives instead of blessings.

Another important reason we should walk in righteousness is to make good use of the Power and Authority which has been given to us by God. The principal weapon that God has given us to use, in order to unleash the power of his authority, is the weapon of Prayer! It is through the power of prayer that we are able bring the perfect will of God down to earth. It is through the power of prayer that we allow God to operate over our situation. It is through the power of prayer that we can exercise authority over the kingdom of darkness. In other words, it is through the power of prayer that we can access the authority which has been given to us by God, through his Son, Jesus Christ.

Once again, if we look at this concept in reverse, we can see that if we, as children of the living God, walk in a path of disobedience, we cannot use the authority he's given us. Simply put, if we disobey the Word of God, our prayers will not be heard. The power that we have when we intercede is blocked or detained when we are walking in disobedience. We are unable to operate in the supernatural realm when we are disobeying God's Word. Prayer is what allows us to access God's supernatural realm, which in turn, gives us the power to speak over our situations.

I hope this may give you a better idea why the enemy is always trying to persuade us to walk in disobedience. The enemy is not after us directly. He is after the Authority and Dominion that we carry because of our relationship with God! The enemy knows that if he can somehow cut off our relationship with God, we become lost and thus, become easy targets for him to use his evil works against us.

Let's never forget the fact that the only purpose of the devil is to destroy God's people. It is just as important to remember that if we do allow ourselves to walk in disobedience, we are stripped of the power to undo the evil works of the kingdom of darkness.

CHAPTER 8

S tand firm then, with the belt of truth buckled around your waist, with the breastplate of righteousness in place. (Eph. 6:14 NIV)

In the 6th chapter of Ephesians, the Apostle Paul talks to us about "spiritual armor" and the important reasons why we, as believers, must learn how to use it.

> For our struggle is not against flesh and blood, but against the rulers, against the authorities, against the power of this dark world and against the spiritual forces of evil in the heavenly realms. (Eph. 6:12 NIV)

This verse specifically tells us that our battles are not physical, but spiritual. Therefore, the only way to fight them and be victorious over them is to fight them in the spirit. In other words, when we make the conscious decision to take up arms against the enemy, we must learn how to properly use these spiritual weapons so they can insure us victory. Our weapons aren't physical weapons, like guns and bombs, but spiritual weapons, like prayer and intercession. Our real battles are fought in the spiritual realm, not in our physical one.

In Ephesians 6, Paul gives us a detailed account of what these weapons are, how far-reaching they can be and how to use them more effectively. The primary and strongest spiritual weapon mentioned by Paul is the weapon of righteousness. In Ephesians 6:14, Paul clearly states that righteousness is the "breastplate" of the believer. Essentially, righteousness is what guarantees us believers divine protection over our lives.

This definition places righteousness in a vitally important position when it comes to spiritual warfare. If we weren't adequately protected by the shield of righteousness, it would be impossible to emerge out of a battle without a serious wound. In other words, it would be impossible to obtain a victory over the kingdom of darkness, if we weren't protected by the righteousness of God's kingdom. Likewise, if we chose not to operate in God's righteousness, we would then be subject to the whims of the kingdom of darkness. We would be vulnerable to the evil schemes of the enemy and become an easy target, preventing us from reaching our earthly purpose.

Because of this, it is vitally important for us to keep our "breastplate" firmly in place in order to preserve our lives and survive the spiritual battles. By seeking and living in God's righteousness, we are able to maintain a victorious upper hand against the kingdom of darkness.

> Therefore, put on the full armor of God, so that when the day comes, you may be able to stand your ground, and after you have done everything, to stand. Stand firm then, with the breastplate of righteousness in place, and with your feet fitted with the readiness that comes from the gospel of peace. In addition to all this, take up the shield of faith, with which you can extinguish all the flaming arrows of the evil one. Take the helmet of salvation and the sword of the Spirit, which is the Word of God. (Eph. 6:13-17 NIV)

Ultimately, this means that we can be in the Gospel (our fitted shoes), have salvation (our helmet), read and accept the Word of God (our sword), and yet, are not walking in righteousness, we are totally exposed, naked and vulnerable to satan and his attacks. This will actually prevent us from operating in the dimensions of authority, dominion, prosperity, healing and deliverance, which our Heavenly Father has destined for all of us.

Knowing all these dynamics of the spirit world, we must recognize the importance of making a solid decision to walk in righteousness. Even though the world gives us a choice of going back and forth between light and darkness, as faithful believers, we cannot afford the luxury of vacillating between accepting or rejecting the choice to walk in righteousness.

Just to be clear, God has guaranteed us a life of victory, and a fulfillment of our destiny in him, but only if we choose to walk the path of his righteousness. Another negative effect of not walking the path of righteousness, is that we lose ourpaternal rights as children of the living God. Simply put, we are removed from our rightful inheritance as God's children and consequently lose all the benefits that stem from that inheritance.

> This is how we know who the children of God are and who the children of the devil are: "Anyone who does not do what is right is not a child of God; nor is anyone who does not love his brother." (1 John 3:10 NIV)

Being sons and daughters of the living God is what gives us the right and authority to operate in the same dimensions as him! This close relationship with our Creator is what places us within his government and allows us to rule over all of creation, which includes exercising authority over the kingdom of darkness.

Additionally, as God's children, we are given access to his throne of grace so we can be forgiven and receive his mercy.

We are also heard by God, and given the ability to govern through prayer and to receive answers when we pray, however, "your iniquities have separated you from your God; your sins have hidden his face from you, so that he will not hear" (Isa. 59:2 NIV).

I hope I have made it clear that when we decide to operate in unjust ways, we are automatically removed from our divine paternity and inheritance, which then removes us from any power or authority we had when we were walking in the path of righteousness. We also need to remember that once we are on this crooked path, we become ambassadors for the evil spirit of injustice, as well as the kingdom of darkness he belongs to. This situation then allows the kingdom of darkness to influence, control and direct our entire lives.

Given everything we've covered up to now, I would also like to clarify the fact that we cannot say that we are children of the living God and at the same time be operating under the spirit of injustice. This would be the perfect definition of an oxymoron. In other words, it is impossible to serve two masters!

> No one can serve two masters. Either he will hate the one and love the other, or he will be devoted to the one and despise the other. You cannot serve God and Money. (Matt. 6:24 NIV).

Remember that we represent God's kingdom of Righteousness, and since no one has seen the Father, it is vital that we reflect the image of his character here on earth. This is truly an amazing and serious commitment for us all. This is why it is imperative that we, as God's physical representation here on earth, walk and behave in righteousness! We must not fall into the sick and unjust parameters of oppressing the poor, allowing or spreading racism, exploiting foreign-born people,permitting slavery and human trafficking, spreading false testimonies, living for material ambitions and all the other perversions that are predominant in the kingdom of darkness.

> In the same way, let your light shine before men, that they may see your good deeds and praise your Father in heaven. (Matt. 5:16 NIV)

As God's children and faithful believers, it is also vitally important that we expand the kingdom of God here on earth. But the interesting conundrum lies in the fact that we must first bring God's kingdom down to earth. You may ask, "How can this important task be done?" It is accomplished by learning as much as we can about all the rules and regulations that govern God's kingdom, and making sure that we are applying them to our lives. Then, we can go out into the world and spread this good news of the kingdom of God to the four corners of the earth!

We should not ever be faking our desire to be righteous. *We should not ever be faking our righteousness.*

> Be careful not to do your 'acts of righteousness' before men, to be seen by them. If you do, you will have no reward from your Father in heaven. (Matt. 6:1 NIV)

We should not practice righteousness based on ulterior motives that have evil intentions behind them. In other words, we shouldn't try to act more saintly, or more "Christian," than those around us, just to satisfy our own personal motives or goals. When the Pharisees practiced their own ideas of righteousness, they felt superior to those around them, and in their own minds they were trying to gain passage to heaven through these works,

Another way that we can approach this simple concept is by not using the acts of righteousness in order to seek the applause or approval of others. This attention would essentially be a reward in our favor. We cannot make the mistake of deciding to operate under the influence of righteousness simply for the self-aggrandizement for our own agendas (Matt. 6:1).

If we really want to bring God's kingdom of righteousness down to earth, we must show the same motivations that Jesus showed when he came to this earth over 2,000 years ago. The motivation Jesus had was based on the immense*love* he had for humanity. Incidentally, love happens to be the main principle of God's kingdom and his light.

One of the most outstanding characteristics of Jesus was his *compassion*. This is why the Bible, on many, many occasions, uses the phrase, "Jesus was moved by compassion." We clearly see that every act of righteousness performed by Jesus while on this earth, was truly made because of his compassion towards us, and not for notoriety or for his own self-aggrandizing agenda.

In God's kingdom, all acts of righteousness must be preceded by compassion. But it is impossible to experience love and compassion when we have hardened hearts or are lacking in forgiveness or are even filled with the roots of bitterness caused by some unrighteous act that we suffered in the past.

This is where divine deliverance comes into play and why it is so important in our walk with God. If we truly want to operate within the parameters of righteousness and be moved by the correct motivating factors, we must first be freed from all damaging roots left by the malignant spirit of injustice. We cannot reach true freedom from these evil spirits just by praying the prayer of renouncement and deliverance found in this book, although that is an excellent place to start. We also need to seek the presence of the Holy Spirit and invite him into our lives, to guide us with the same compassion Jesus had. We can conclude that Jesus is the best role model to follow if we are indeed serious in wanting to be faithful followers of his message and legacy.

CHAPTER 9

Not only does the operation of the spirit of injustice have an impact on our physical and spiritual lives, it also takes a huge toll on our emotions. It becomes virtually impossible to not be directly affected emotionally when we have been attacked by the spirit of injustice. This is because God created each of us with a body, soul and spirit.

Each one of these three components are interrelated with each other, so when one of them is affected positively or negatively, it provokes an impact on the others. This phenomenon explains why churches find themselves filled with gifted individuals who are in deep emotional pain. They are still carrying the emotional wounds of their past! In others words, they are saved but not free.

So, even though we have come to Jesus and have made all the commitments to be saved, we still feel the weight of the wounds that have been inflicted on us by the devil, by the world and often by the very poor decisions we had made in our lives.

Let's look at the emotional ramifications that occur when we are attacked by the spirit of injustice. The emotional symptoms that are most evident are signs of total apathy for life itself, hatred toward everything, resentment, roots of bitterness, and depression (that is, the loss of love for the things that used to bring us joy and pleasure). Another emotional indicator is difficulty in finding happiness or in trusting others, low self-esteem (which is a very poor opinion of oneself), a great rejection of others, hatred against God and His Word and an enormous disbelief that God really loves them and wants the best for them.

Another common emotional sign is guilt. This symptom is extremely self-destructive because the person affected thinks that everything is their fault and that because they were involved in the circumstances, they must deserve whatever ishappening to them. Often, people who have been a victim of the evil cycles of the spirit of injustice believe that what they are going through is the result of God being angry and punishing them. This may stem from the idea that God has not yet forgiven them for a past sin they have committed.

I think that I must clear up the fact that this sense of guilt or condemnation is not because the person has little faith, but perhaps because the believer is dealing with issues of low self-esteem. Because of their bad past experiences, many believers have such a reduced sense of self-value that it's very hard for them to truly experience the magnitude of God's love for them. The reason for this is often that they've never experienced genuine unconditional love from the people around them. Thus, for the mere fact that they don't have a reference point for any comparison, receiving true unconditional love is actually something foreign to them and it's difficult for them to truly receive God's love and acceptance.

Another reason for low self-esteem, could be that the person has suffered sexual abuse from someone they trusted, like a parent or parent figure. They might have also been abandoned by a person that promised "forever love" to them, again by a parent, for example. This can extend to physical and emotional abuse by one's spouse, where time and again, the person attempts to trust their loved one, and time and again, they are vehemently and intentionally betrayed.

The final result is that all these people end up thinking that they are not worthy of forgiveness or unconditional love from a God who genuinely cares for them. All these reasons I've mentioned make it even more vital to be able to properly identify the works of the spirit of injustice, and the emotional consequences it leaves in its wake. It is just as important for people who have been affected by this evil spirit to take the time to get healed through a process of inner healing and deliverance.

You may remember when I mentioned the fact that the prayer of renouncement is indispensable for the cases we have just mentioned. Not only does this powerful prayer cut off the roots of these evil spirits, but it also serves to free oneself of the emotional wounds, caused by their evil operations. Many times, the people who have been under attack by this sneaky spirit, don't actually know what the extent of their emotional damage really is. This is where we must seek the presence of the Holy Spirit, so he can guide us to all truth. By exposing the truth, the Holy Spirit will also expose the roots or any marks left by the slimy spirit, so we can be completely freed from its attacks.

Seven Steps to Healing Our Emotions

In order to prepare ourselves for these seven steps, we must first go through some preliminary warm ups. We must begin by freeing ourselves from the spirit of injustice. We do this by renewing our faith and confessing our sins to Jesus Christ. We need to accept him as if we were just beginning our walk with him. We make our confession of faith and we accept Jesus as our only Savior. Let's not forget that we cannot have authority over an evil spirit unless we partake of the redeeming power of Christ's blood. The only way this can happen is by converting to Christ Jesus and by asking him to forgive our sin. Secondly, we need to continue a more detailed and in-depth confession of our sins, asking God to forgive us for each one. Then we need to forgive all those in our lives who have been under the influence of the spirit of injustice and that have caused us all that pain. Following this, we need to pray out loud the prayers of renouncement and deliverance found inside this book. Once we have completed these preliminary warm up steps, we are ready to initiate the seven steps for our inner healing process.

1. First step: Accept God's forgiveness

    "If we confess our sins, he is faithful and just and will forgive us our sins and purify us from all unrighteousness" (1 John 1:9 NIV).

One of the most difficult things to do after we've fallen into and been wounded by recurring sinful ways, is to accept the fact that God has already forgiven us. His forgiveness covers *all* types of sin, from murder and prostitution toseemingly insignificant "white lies."

Most often, because of our ignorance of the full redeeming power of Christ's blood and sometimes because of issues of our low self-esteem, we continue to carry a cross that has already been lifted from us long time ago by the infinite love of Jesus Christ!

As the accuser of the brethren, the enemy constantly incriminates us, reminding us of sins we have committed in the past which God has already forgiven us for. The only reason the enemy gets away with this it that we allow it. We allow this guilt to hold us in bondage, taking our faults out of proportion, far beyond their true dimensions. The accuser grinds away at our thoughts, forcing us to see our sins as overwhelmingly large and even unforgivable, thus guiding us to doubt the unconditional love of God.

This is why it is imperative for us to redirect our mind-set in how we perceive our own identities in Christ, and then reset our perceptions as to how we portray our Heavenly Father. In other words, we need to renew our minds to the levels and stature of our perfect role model, Jesus Christ.

2. Second step: Change the way you think

> "Do not conform any longer to the patterns of this world, but be transformed by the renewing of your mind. Then you will be able to test and approve what God's will is--his good, pleasing and perfect will" (Rom. 12:2 NIV).

The most traumatic experiences that we face as human beings, in my opinion, don't just affect our physical bodies, but are even harder hitting to our emotions. And this impact on our emotions then goes on to affect our perceptions. In other words, our negative experiences cause a deep emotional impact that changes how we see ourselves and how we see our surrounding world.

Emotional traumas provoke certain changes in an individual's perspectives, and the best way to treat these traumas is through what is known as cognitive therapy. These therapies are specially designed to help the individual with their emotional traumas by assisting them in learning new habits, helping them find healthy channels to vent their frustrations, and actually discover new perceptions of their surrounding world.

This is why it is so important to recognize the fact that if we truly want to heal the damages caused by the spirit of injustice, we first must begin by changing the way we perceive ourselves and the way we perceive God. To accomplish this vital task, we must stop blaming others and begin to take responsibility for our own misdeeds. In other words, we must indulge in the exercise of self-reflection, owning up to our actions without continuing to condemn ourselves for them. It often occurs that the worst punishers that exist are those punishers that are within us!

It may help us to better understand the difficult things we've gone through by realizing that the enemy only attacks people who possess a huge potential for God. As the saying goes, no one robs an empty vault. This is why it's so important to recognize the need to rid oneself of all feelings of guilt. Guilt is the only grip the enemy has on you that can keep you from reaching your full potential in God. It's precisely because the enemy knows what God thinks of you and how much authority you carry as God's child, that it keeps trying to attack you, so you cast doubt over your authority, losing your capability to undo its evil works.

If we really want to heal our emotions we must look to God's Word and read what God says about us. Remember, if we want to change our thoughts and behaviors, we must first learn new habits. More often than not, we are extremely diligent in finding out what people and the world think about us, but we fail in searching out what God says about us.

By not searching for God and his infinite wisdom, we are stuck with building our own self-esteem with the comments and perceptions of the people surrounding us, which are often negative, unjust and cruel. In other words, all ofthe feelings that we've based our identity of "self" on, are generated in a system with values and criteria stemming from very questionable interests. We need to base our identity on true values that are pure and transparent; the values that govern the kingdom of light. If we build up our self-esteem on human and earthly criteria, it would be like building a house on top of the sand.

> Therefore, everyone who hears these words of mine and puts them into practice is like a wise man who built his house on a rock. (Matt. 7:24 NIV)

To recap, we need to understand that as born-again Christians, the right way to live our lives is to base the perceptions of ourselves on what God thinks and says about us, and not in what people think.

How can we know what God thinks about us? The way we can know what God has already said about us is by the reading of God's Word, the Bible. In order to remove ourselves from the mind-set of failure, insecurity, fear, pain, frustration and all other negative thoughts, we need to set aside some quality time to read the Bible, to nourish our spirits and minds with God's Word. The more we know about and believe in what God has said about us, the less we will believe the lies of the devil and its constant attempts to influence our minds.

3. Third step: Be careful what you say

    "The tongue has the power of life and death, and those who love it will eat its fruits" (Prov. 18:21 NIV).

Part of the process of renewing our thoughts and learning new habits, lies in the importance of being more careful with what we say.

    But the things that come out of the mouth come from the heart, and these make a man 'unclean.' (Matt. 15:18 NIV)

It is quite common for people who are filled with pain to lash out against others around them, consciously or unconsciously. In other cases, they simply find themselves constantly talking about their own dismal situations.

The act of constantly talking in a compulsive way could be a sign of deep anxiety, used as a coping mechanism to provide an outlet for their negative emotions. By the way, it's easy to see what's really going on inside a person's mind, simply by listening to what that they're really saying. It is very common for people who have been wounded emotionally, to use disgruntled words, complaints, cursed words, words of criticism, judgmental words or even negative words about themselves, or others. It is much like an escape valve, that the person uses to release the pressure caused by the frustration of their emotional pain.

It is somewhat alarming that as loyal servants of Jesus Christ, we are unaware of the enormous power our words possess. We are often unaware that our words have the power to fortify the cycles of oppression, just as they have the power to free us from those same cycles.

If we truly want to rid ourselves of our emotional pain, we need to stop complaining and stop repeating our sob stories to everyone we meet. The main reason people go around telling their tragic stories, is to create an atmosphere of commiseration, commonly known as a desperate desire to promote self pity in the eyes of others. The objective of this frantic desire is to hopefully stimulate some sort of empathy, or simply play the eternal victimization card to anyone who will listen.

This self-victimization can be also used as a way to try and legitimize or excuse their irresponsible and neglectful behavior. It also serves as an excuse to not progress in their lives, because they are perpetually living in the past. It's almost as if their lives consist only of reliving their tragic experiences of the past, and that's all they will know for the rest of their lives. These individuals seem to have imprisoned themselves in their own tragedies.

In summary, if we truly want to leave the vicious cycle of past traumas behind us, then it is imperative that we stop reinforcing those cycles with our continual negative talk. We have to stop referring only to those past traumatic events. We need to stop saying things like:

"I am just not happy anymore."

"This tragedy completely destroyed me and I'll never be able to recuperate from it."

"If only he hadn't done that to me. It's so unfair!"

As long as we continue expressing these statements of defeat, we will continue to strengthen those cycles of trauma and emotional pain. However, let me clarify that it's something completely different to confide our story one time to a parent, or even a close friend, just to be able to unload the heavy burden of what caused you so much grief. What I do want to caution you about, is not to use the telling of your story just to gain sympathy and pity, and especially not to use it as an excuse to act negligently. Another vital word of caution is that you must not discuss your situations with anyone that really can't help you to solve them.

4. Fourth step: Talk to God

Taking time out to pray to God is indispensable for maintaining our emotional healing. It is truly therapeutic for us to be able to unload our troubles to the only one who loves us in such an awesome and unconditional manner. As our Creator, God is the only one that truly knows us, and he wants us to share our pain, our fears, our insecurities, and our frustrations with him, and trust him to heal those areas.

My recommendation is that you not limit your conversation with God to just a few minutes a day, but to truly invest some quality time with him. This means that we should seek God's presence, sharing in an intimate relationship with him by opening our hearts to him, and to get to know his heart; to simply cry out in his presence. This is really the kind of relationship that we should be seeking with our Heavenly Father and Creator.

Our best example of this special relationship can be found in Jesus. Jesus didn't just pray three times a day, as the custom was in the Jewish faith. Jesus would retreat to the mountains for weeks at a time to be in intimacy with his Heavenly Father. It is also as important to seek a close friendship with the Holy Spirit if we truly want to be healed on the inside. Let us never forget that it is the Holy Spirit who heals our wounds and who also reveals the heart of the Father. It it vital to realize that when we truly want complete and optimum spiritual and emotional healing, we must develop an intimate relationship with God the Father, God the Son, and God the Holy Spirit. And we can only fulfill this task by spending quality time with them.

5.   Fifth step: Be extremely careful who you are talking to

"Do not be misled: 'Bad company corrupts good character" (1 Cor. 15:33 NIV).

Unfortunately, when we are going through some painful, emotional things, we often prefer to develop relationships with people who indirectly celebrate our pain, and not with those who could better motivate us to emerge from them. As the saying goes, "misery loves company." In order to heal our emotional pains, we must always try to surround ourselves with people who are positive and full of faith. We must look for those who will help us motivate ourselves in reaching the next level of our lives and will share words of encouragement, and not listen to our whining. In other words, we need to seek out people of faith who will empower us to advance and reach the destiny God has designed for us.

Another good tool that we can use to combat all this negativity, is having a good support group. It is a well known fact that people who have gone through addiction rehabilitation, or have suffered a personal and traumatic event in their lives, are able to respond quite well to what is commonly known as "group therapy" or "support group". The dynamics of this concept are to gather up an assembly of people who have gone through a similar ordeal as yourself, and basically share their experiences with you and the rest of the group, with the final objective being a better understanding of your own situation. Sometimes it can be helpful just to know you're not alone. Listening to others who have gone through what you've gone through, allows you to receive a better understanding of your own situation and find a way to overcome your psychological trauma, through the more complete experiences of others in the support group.

We need to stress the fact that when we are going through some difficult life events, we should reach out for help and not keep harboring the burdens of our trauma within ourselves. However, we need to make sure that the person or peoplewe are reaching out to are qualified to give us positive and sound advice. We must never fall into believing that we are wise in our own opinion, and we have the necessary means to solve our own traumatic experiences by ourselves. Some sort of therapy is always recommended, and in some severe cases, it should be required.

Fortunately, in most of today's churches we can find these very vital and important support groups. The great advantage of seeking emotional help in a church setting, is the fact that the leaders of these groups are born-again Christians who count on the guidance and assistance of the Holy Spirit. These spiritual elements are what will guarantee us a true healing process, as well as a permanent one because, "if the Son sets you free, you will be free indeed" (John 8:36 NIV).

6. Sixth step: Help others

The Bible says that everything that the enemy does to harm us, God will turn it into something good for us (Rom. 8:28). Having said this, it is still up to us to choose whether we want to be victims our whole life, or whether we want to be victorious in Christ Jesus. This is, by far, the most important decision we can make for ourselves, and no matter how much someone loves us, we are the only ones that can make this decision.

Another very good technique we can use to heal our broken emotions, is to share the story of how we overcame our own negative experiences to help others in the same situation. This will let them make their own comparisons and come to their own conclusions. In this technique, two powerful things happen. First, it helps the person with the experience already under control, to use their retelling as their own retro healing therapy. It re-emphasizes all the basic concepts that caused their inner healing to happen, as well as being a self-motivational factor. Second, it helps the person who is still going through those things to understand that healing is a available, and can be a reality in their situation as well,

I always recommend that anyone truly searching for emotional healing should involve themselves in some sort of activity, like a church project or community work. In that way, they would be able to help people that might be going through similar situations. In other words, by helping to heal other people's wounds, we are simultaneously helping to heal our own wounds. When you share your testimony with others, make sure you are doing it to show how God's love can restore a broken heart, and not to gain attention or self-pity.

7. Seventh step: Discover your purpose!

The one thing we as Christians must know for sure is that we were all created by God with a purpose. We all have a mission to complete on earth, even though we've have gone through, or are currently going through, some difficult things. This is absolutely a concept you can take to the bank! The main proof of this is that despite everything you've gone through, you are still alive! As the saying goes, if you're still breathing, God's not done! You are here for a reason. God has a purpose for your pain, and what you are going through is not to destroy you but to serve as your testimony!

One of the most important things we can ask ourselves is, "How can I find out what God's purpose is for my life?" We can begin by understanding that our purpose is very closely related to our inherent potential. In other words, that special ability that is uniquely yours and makes you different from others. I think that the best way that you can find out this is by asking those people who know you very well and who genuinely appreciate you, what they consider your potential. What it is that we can do that flows naturally from us and feels nearly effortless? What is it that we can do which is so pleasing to others?

Another great resource we can use to discover our purpose is seeking the revelation of the Holy Spirit. All we need to do is to pray so that the Holy Spirit may guide us to this truth. Always remember that the devil will try to get you to turn your back on your God-given purpose. We also must know that one of the main assignments of the spirit of injustice is to try and distort our self-image so we don't recognize the potential given to us by God to fulfill our earthly mission. The enemy knows that if we discover our full potential, that will lead us to discover our purpose, and when we start walking in our purpose, we then start walking with authority. That fact represents a clear threat to the kingdom of darkness.

When we are confident in who we are as children of God, and we know where we are going, we stop accepting anything from the kingdom of darkness that might distract us from our purpose. The point remains that the devil wants to distract and distance us from our place of destiny, fulfillment and prosperity. In other words, the enemy wants to do everything it can to keep us from the "promised land" that God has prepared for us.

What makes all these things so relevant is the fact that we were not put in this world to have perfect lives, completely free of all negative situations, but rather to try and live our lives with purpose, *despite* all the negative situations we may be going through. We should not be pondering how many times we have fallen, but how many times we have gotten back up and continued walking forward.

Our real challenge as servants of the Almighty God, is to embrace the example of Jesus Christ and walk with him to our divine destiny, convinced of the fact that all things are possible in Christ, who is the one that gives us the strength to continue!

CHAPTER 10

If there exists something that competes directly with what God has said about us, it would be all the bad situations we have to live through. It becomes extremely difficult to see ourselves as God sees us, when we go through such difficult things including painful hardships, demeaning rejections, and even slavery. This is exactly why God has asked us to walk by faith and not by sight. In reality, we often find ourselves living a world that seems quite the opposite of the truth of God's kingdom and the things he has promised us.

One thing is for certain: the spirit of injustice can have a devastating impact on our emotions. Consequently, it also tries to ruin our true identity in Christ. Notice that when we are hit by any traumatic and painful experience, the first thing we resort to is questioning everything and blaming everyone.

We lock ourselves into a small box of self-pity and we forget everything God has said about us, that we are the apple of his eye, that we are a blessed nation, that we are high priests, that we are a chosen people and that we are more than conquerors. The only thing that pops into our minds is why this is happening to us if God loves us and is supposed to be our protector. We ignore that the fact that the root of our problem isn't from God, but from the kingdom of darkness.

In order that satan might not outwit us. For we
are not unaware of his schemes. (2 Cor. 2:11 NIV)

My people are destroyed from lack of knowledge.
(Hos. 4:6 NIV)

It becomes increasingly difficult for us to stay firm in the
Word of God when so many bad things are happening around
us and to us, but it's not impossible. Our relief lies in the fact
that God will not ask us to do anything that Jesus, our best
example, hasn't done already. If there was anyone who was
relentlessly attacked by the spirit of injustice, it was Jesus!
He was even betrayed by one of his own disciples, his good
friend Judas. Jesus was also falsely accused of doing miracles
in the name of demonic deities, of being a false prophet and of
causing public unrest (in those days, causing public unrest was
such a terrible crime that it was punishable by death).

Jesus was humiliated for being an Israelite and for his
poor social status. Jesus was born in the very poor village of
Nazareth (which had a meager population of about 400), and
he was the son of a carpenter (which in those days, was of
the lowest job status). Jesus was also ridiculed for speaking
humble Aramaic, instead of the cultured language of high
society Greek.

Jesus received plenty of unjust ridicule and rejection
because of the people he surrounded himself with: lepers, the
terminally ill, prostitutes, children and women who had been
shunned by their husbands. Jesus was constantly mocked and
slandered for selecting smelly fishermen to be his disciples.
Judas, was the only exception, who was a tax collector before
he joining the ministry as its official treasury accountant.

Jesus spent his adult life being constantly rejected, even
though all he ever did was spread love and good deeds. No one
would accept, or give any credit to, a man from Nazareth and
who was born a Jew. Jesus also knew firsthand the feeling of

abandonment, when his closest friend, Peter, denied knowing him three times, and when all the other disciples scattered in fear of losing their own lives, leaving him to hang on the cross and die alone (with the exception of a few faithful women).

Jesus also suffered the early loss of his dear friend Lazarus. He was also falsely charged, judged and convicted to die, without having committed any crime whatsoever! Finally, Jesus was tortured, humiliated and executed, as a common criminal. Jesus suffered all these afflictions to establish a more equitable and just society, and to provide a pathway to free ourselves from the oppressing influences of the spirit of injustice.

Never once did all these circumstances cause Jesus to surrender the core identity that God the Father had given to him. Jesus had more than enough reasons to doubt his identity. But he never once wavered! Jesus knew exactly who was behind all the attacks, uprisings and erroneous judgments. He knew it was generated by the kingdom of darkness. Again, Jesus was very clear about the fact that the enemy wasn't so much after him, but was after the anointing that he carried as the Son of God. Satan knew that if he could somehow trick him into giving up that power, then Jesus would be giving up his grip over satan and his evil works.

However, Jesus was continually steadfast and confident that as the Son of God, his calling was not to be a victim of the struggles caused by the kingdom of darkness and its unjust government, but rather to fight against it and defeat it!

> He who does what is sinful is of the the devil, because the devil has been sinning from the beginning. (1 John 3:8 NIV)

Jesus was well aware of the fact that the kingdom of darkness would go after our identity, to try to change our minds and have us question what God has said about us. The devil knows that if it can accomplish this task, it will essentially have stopped us from using our authority over it. Let's not forget that this authority has been given to us through the death of Jesus Christ on the cross.

We see clear evidence of the devil's attempts to get Jesus to fall for his lying temptations in Luke 4:1-13. The important thing to note here is that nearly all of the temptations that the devil made to Jesus were aimed directly at Jesus's identity.

> The devil said to him, 'If you are the Son of God,
> tell this stone to become bread.' (Luke 4:3 NIV)

When we hear the devil saying to Jesus, "If you are the Son of God," he is trying to place doubt into Jesus' thoughts of the validity of who he really is. Not only did Jesus rebuke the evil influence of the devil, but he counterattacked it by using the Word of God the Father, when he answered, "It is written: Man does not live on bread alone'" (Luke 4;4 NIV).

Satan continued to try even harder when he next said, "I will give you all their authority and splendor, for it has been given to me, and I can give it to anyone I want to. So if you worship me, it will all be yours" (Luke 4:6-7 NIV). In other words, satan was still trying to make a deal with Jesus, for something that already belonged to him. All satan was attempting to do with Jesus was get him to question the glory and the power that he already had as the Son of God. However, since Jesus was well aware of satan's evil intentions, he counterattacked by rebuking satan out of his life forever!

> Jesus answered, "It is written: 'Worship the Lord
> your God and serve him only.'" (Luke 4:8 NIV)

When satan realized that he was getting nowhere fast, he took a different approach by twisting some promises that God has made to all of us, found in Psalms 91.

The devil led him to Jerusalem and had him stand on the highest point of the temple. 'If you are the Son of God,' he said, 'throw yourself down from here. For it is written: 'He will command his angels concerning you to guard you carefully; they will lift you up in their hands, so that you will not strike your foot against a stone.' (Luke 4:9-11, NIV)

As we can clearly see, satan knows exactly what God thinks of us, as well as all the promises he has in store for us. Satan will also do everything in his power, to keep us from receiving those promises. The point is that we cannot allow the enemy to gain any influence over our thoughts or have us doubt our identity in Christ. As children of God, if this occurs, it would automatically impede our ability to operate in our God-given authority against the kingdom of darkness and over all its unjust works.

While satan was tempting Jesus, not only did Jesus not turn the rock into bread, but he also counterattacked satan when he tempted Jesus to throw himself off the cliff.

Jesus answered, "It is said: 'Do not put the Lord your God to the test.'" (Luke 4:12 NIV)

If Jesus had yielded to satan, then satan would automatically have had the power to exercise authority over him. This is why Jesus never backed down. This principle also works for us as children of God. When we yield to the devil's lies, we automatically open the spiritual doors of our lives to him, so he can operate freely and have total authority over us.

Even though we saw a temporary stop in satan's attack on Jesus, the devil kept hovering over him, right up to the end of Jesus' life on earth. Even though satan was never successful in tricking Jesus, that never stopped him from trying. We see this up to the final moments of Jesus, while he was hanging on the cross. Satan used the thief on Jesus' left to try and tempt him one last time.

One of the criminals who hung there hurled insults to him: "Aren't you the Christ? Save yourself and us!" (Luke 23:39 NIV)

But since Jesus already knew the evil works of the devil, He paid it no mind and ignored the comment completely. Jesus did, however, allow the thief on his right to defend him and his righteous identity when he said, "We are punished justly, for we are getting what our deeds deserve. But this man has done nothing wrong"(Luke 24:41 NIV). Jesus did respond to this thief, and with words that reaffirmed his identity as the Son of God.

Jesus answered him, "I tell you the truth, today you will be with me in paradise.' (Luke 23: 43 NIV).

Jesus was demonstrating the fact that even though it looked like he was defeated, and about to die in the most horrible manner, he never allowed his circumstances to change his essence and identity. In a way, he was saying, "My identity does not depend upon the situation I'm going through, nor does it depend on what others think about me. My identity depends solely on what my God has already said about me!"

I can only imagine what might have gone through the mind of Jesus, Perhaps thoughts like: "Even in the most difficult times of my life on earth, I will let the devil know that I am truly the Son of God and that there is nothing the kingdom of darkness can do about that reality." This is how God expects us to act as his children and as followers of Jesus. We must face the attacks of the enemy head on, and we must never allow our circumstances to determine our identity.

Declare this with me out loud:

> I declare that my identity is not dependent on my circumstances, nor is it dependent on my past, nor in what others think about me. My identity depends on what God has already said about

me. I also declare that nothing the kingdom of darkness tries to do against me will change this reality in my life, in Jesus name!

We need to make sure that when we declare anything, as we are standing in the kingdom of light, we first must be conscious of who we are in God's kingdom, and recognize the immense value that Jesus left for us at the cross. Jesus not only died on the cross to redeem us from sin, he also died for our deliverance, our healing and most of all, to give us a new identity in him. So, let me reiterate that it doesn't really matter what we identified with in the past, what we've done, what horrific circumstances we've had to face, nor does it even matter what wounds, scars or labels the spirit of injustice might have inflicted upon us. Once we are born-again as Christians, we must always stand firm, with full consciousness of new identity in Christ Jesus!

Let's also remember that God's perfect plan for us is still on course and hasn't changed one bit. But above all, it is indispensable to accept the redeeming love of God, and know that he wants to restore everything that the enemy has tried to destroy in our lives. All God wants for us is to give us a new beginning! No matter what we have gone through, God still wants what is best for us.

Everything that God has said about us in the Bible is absolute and there is nothing that can stand up against it or nullify it. We will always be the apple of his eye, we will always be his chosen and redeemed people, the light of the world, and the salt of the earth. If you truly believe this, then declare the following declaration of identity in an audible voice, in the name of Jesus!

DECLARATION OF NEW IDENTITY IN CHRIST

I declare that I am a child of the living God and as such, I am entitled to be a co-inheritor with Jesus Christ to all the benefits of his kingdom.

I accept the paternity of my Heavenly Father, through his Son Jesus Christ. I declare that I am sitting next to him in celestial places. I declare that I'm an inheritor of God's kingdom, and therefore, have direct access to his throne of grace. I declare that each one of God's promises belongs to me, and I now accept them all in my life.

I accept that I am unconditionally loved by my Heavenly Father and that I have been justified by him through my faith. I accept that all my sins have been forgiven and that all stains of my past have been erased.

According to 1 Peter 2:9, I declare that I am a chosen generation, a royal priesthood, and a holy nation. I accept the fact that I have been removed from the kingdom of darkness, into the admirable light of Jesus!

I rebuke and renounce all labels, or vile names, given to me by the kingdom of darkness, by society, by family members or by friends. I no longer accept them in my life and I cancel them, in the name of Jesus Christ!

I cancel all names I have used in the past that weren't aligned with the identity God has given me. I cancel all forms of identity that have been transferred to my life through generational curses, through evil assignments, through unjust acts caused by the spirit of injustice, and by bad attitudes I have acquired consciously or unconsciously. I rebuke all thoughts of failure, condemnation, feelings of depression, frustration, and poor concepts of myself.

I cancel all negative and evil entities that have been activated in my life through trauma I've suffered in my childhood through physical and emotional abuse caused by people in

117

authority over my life. I nullify all emotional scars caused by the spirit of injustice, in Jesus name!

I make null and void all false identities that have entered my life through the ill effects of low self-esteem, insecurity, fear of rejection, or bias against my gender, race, social status or nationality. I declare them all inoperable in my life, in the name of Jesus Christ!

I accept the new identity given to me through Jesus Christ and his death on the cross. I also accept the fact that I have been redeemed by the blood of Jesus, that his favor is upon me and that I am a new creation in him.

I declare that I was created to govern, that I have been anointed to prosper and I have been empowered to be victorious and to possess what God has reserved for me. I believe that I can do all things through Christ who strengthens me.

I declare and accept the fact that I am the salt of the earth, the light of the world, the bride of the lamb, the apple of God's eye, and that my body is the temple of the Holy Spirit.

I now accept that I'm God's chosen generation and am justified by Christ Jesus. I am a warrior in God's divine army, a sheep of his flock and a disciple for Jesus. I am a co-inheritor with Christ Jesus.

I accept the fact that I have the mind of Christ and that his wisdom is in me. I confirm that I am blessed and therefore all of my endeavors shall prosper.

I declare that I am filled with faith, and that the fruits of the Holy Spirit dwell within me. I declare that I have been justified by my faith in Jesus, declared sanctified through his forgiveness, and have been washed by the blood of Jesus Christ.

I now accept the strength that comes from the Holy Spirit, and therefore am strong enough to face and overcome all adversarial circumstances that come my way during my walk on this earth.

I establish the fact that failure has absolutely no place in my life and that I have been equipped by God to be victorious over all situations. I am more than a conqueror through Christ Jesus!

I confess that I am dead to sin, and my flesh has been crucified with Jesus on the cross. I now accept the baptism and anointing of the Holy Spirit.

I will no longer accept fear in my life. I accept and declare that God is for me, not against me. I declare according to Psalms 91 that God's angels are always near me, watching over me and protecting me in all my ways. Therefore, my heart is confident in God.

I accept the fact that I was created in God's image and likeness, and therefore I am his exact replica. I accept that God's breath is within me and that I possess the same divine DNA as my Heavenly Father, to operate in the same dimensions that my Creator operates in.

I now establish that from this day forward, I will be walking by faith, not by sight. I believe that I have been anointed to be prosperous in all areas of my life, that I carry God's divine purpose, and that everything that occurs in my life, will work together for my good.

I accept the new life and authority God has deposited in me to resurrect everything that was once dead around me. I now speak life over my dreams, my projects, my family members, my ministry, my business and everything else that surrounds my life.

I declare and accept the power and dominion that was given to me by God in the garden of Eden, to rule over all circumstances.

I accept the Holy Spirit of God as the exclusive guide of my life. I now give the Holy Spirit total legal authority to reaffirm this new identity that I have through Jesus.

I now make null and void all voices trying to influence my life that are contrary to God's Word, in the mighty name of Jesus! Amen.

CHAPTER 11

For I the Lord, love justice; I hate robbery and iniquity. (Isa. 61:8 NIV)

As I have mentioned before, justice is what forms the base of God's throne. It is also the reason that Jesus came down to earth, and should be the identity seal of every Christian. To practice justice is not only a divine mandate, but most importantly, is a prerequisite to salvation.

For the Lord is righteous, he loves justice; upright men will see his face. (Psa. 11:7 NIV)

This is not a figment of your imagination, nor are you seeing double. The fact is that you are reading correctly! This is what the Bible says about how important it is to be righteous.

For I tell you that unless your righteousness surpasses that of the Pharisees and the teachers of the law, you will certainly not enter the kingdom of heaven. (Matt. 5:16 NIV)

In other words, what Jesus was trying to convey to his people was a very simple concept. Jesus simply said that as his followers, we need to practice justice greater than than which was practiced by the world and those who practiced "religion." You see, the righteousness that was practiced by the Pharisees and the Sadducees during the time of Jesus, was a type of justice that was partial, manipulated and extremely convenient for those in the elite tiers of that society. It was indeed a justice system that conformed to the political rules, the upper social classes and to the strict religious society of those times, and not a justice according to the parameters of God's kingdom.

The only justice that Jesus wanted for his followers was one that was real and fair for everyone, not one based on snobbery, fake attitudes and plenty of personal interests. We know that Jesus was so much against the pompous attitudes of the scribes and Pharisees, that he actually called them "hypocrites" and "whitewashed tombs."

> Woe to you, teachers of the law and Pharisees, you hypocrites! You are like whitewashed tombs, which look beautiful on the outside, but on the inside are full of dead men's bones and everything unclean. In the same way, on the outside you appear to people as righteous, but on the inside, you are full of hypocrisy and wickedness. (Matt. 24:27-28 NIV)

Jesus often used these analogies to teach his disciples to differentiate between the "laws of justice" established by religious heads and local lawmakers, and the the law of justice established by his Father in Heaven. It is important to note that this was one of the primary reasons God sent Jesus to the earth, to re-establish God's divine law on earth, as it is in heaven. As faithful believers, we must all recognize the marked difference between the justice that operates in the world stage, and God's divine justice, which we are called to represent.

Allow me to break it down in a more understandable way. We live in a world where we play the "live and let live" card. This means that we don't pick a fight with our neighbors if they haven't done anything to provoke us. The same goes for not hating someone, if they haven't done anything against us. Finally, we don't become enemies of someone who has been at peace with us. But often we've been taught that if someone has done us harm, that we do have the right to hate them, or maybe even give them some payback because they "deserved it."

However, in God's kingdom, the parameters of his divine righteousness are completely opposite. The Bible tells us to "not be overcome by evil, but overcome evil with good" (Rom. 12:21 NIV). Jesus himself said, "You have heard that it was said, 'Love your neighbor and hate your enemy'. But I tell you: Love your enemies and pray for those who persecute you, that you may be sons of your Father in heaven. He causes his sun to rise on the evil and the good, and sends rain on the righteous and the unrighteous" (Matthew 5:43-45 NIV).

What Jesus is trying to teach us is that what is considered "just conduct" in today's society is not necessarily the truly just conduct of God's kingdom. Therefore, if we really want to practice the righteousness of God's kingdom, the true justice taught to us by Jesus, we must first learn the principles of righteousness found in God's Word, and then learn how to operate in them. Once we are well instructed in these areas, we cannot allow the spirit of injustice to re-enter our lives and start influencing or controlling us ever again.

> Since they did not know the righteousness that comes from God and sought to establish their own, they did not submit to God's righteousness. (Rom. 10:3 NIV)

It is now clear to see that our justice is quite different from God's righteousness. Notice, God does not look at things the way we look at them. It is only God's responsibility to judge us and spread his righteousness to all of us, not the other way around.

> But the Lord said to Samuel, 'Do not consider his appearance or his height, for I have rejected him. The Lord does not look at the things man looks at. Man looks at the outward appearance, but the Lord looks at the heart.'" (1 Sam. 16:7 NIV)

It is for this reason that Jesus told his disciples to love their enemies, to bless those who curse them and to pray for those who persecute them. We know that this was a very hard lesson for them to learn, because they were so used to doing the exact opposite.

That's why we have the saying "Old habits die hard." The Bible actually tells us something very similar:

> If you love those who love you, what reward will you get? Are not the tax collectors doing that? And if you only greet your brother, what are you doing more than others? Do not even pagans do that? Be perfect, therefore, as your Father is perfect. (Matt. 5:46-47 NIV)

As I've mentioned earlier, to operate in righteousness, according to the parameters of God's kingdom, often means that we must do the opposite of what is being dictated by others in society or by our culture. We can even go one step further and say that we'll often have to go contrary to everything we have learned and practiced all our lives. But this is what God's kingdom is all about. He brings us a view of what it's like in his kingdom, and wants to share things like a new culture of respect for one another, more compassion for each other, a new way to forgive one another, a new way to value and love each other. It is precisely this new culture of compassion, forgiveness, and of valuing and loving one another, that God's kingdom brings to us. However, this new culture brings with it a certain amount of conflict as it clashes with the policies of "justice" that are practiced within the human race.

Let's review what the Bible says:

> For I, the Lord, love justice; I hate robbery and iniquity. In my faithfulness I will reward them and make an everlasting covenant with them. (Isa. 61:8 NIV)

God is so understanding toward us, that he is willing to forgive our sins, in proportion to how willing we are to forgive those who offend us.

> For if you forgive men when they sin against you, your Heavenly Father will also forgive you. But if you do not forgive men their sins, your Father will not forgive your sins. (Matt. 6:14-15 NIV)

It is because we find it so hard to forgive others, that the spirit of injustice is able to minister bad things to us such as hatred, lack of forgiveness, and rejection. This is all in an effort to keep us from being forgiven by our Heavenly Father, so we could not have a chance to reach his mercy, and consequently, be unable to live the life of fulfillment that he has promised us.

GOD HATES INJUSTICE

> There are six things the Lord hates, seven that are detestable to him: haughty eyes, a lying tongue, hands that shed innocent blood, a heart that devises wicked schemes, feet that are quick to rush into evil, a false witness who pours out lies and a man who stirs up dissension among brothers. (Prov. 6:16-19 NIV)

These verses just happen to detail all the sins that are associated with the spirit of injustice. These evil practices are directly contrary to God's kingdom and his essence. Having said this, it is still up to all of us as believers to utilize our God-given authority and undo all works of the devil. By doing this we are bringing God's will down to earth and helping to establish his kingdom of righteousness:

> The reason the Son of God appeared was to destroy the devil's work. (1 John 3:8 NIV)

There is a very good reason why God asks us to love one another and even to love our enemies. When we practice true love even for our enemies, we reflect the true essence of God. Love is the key that allows us to operate in sync with God's kingdom, and this opens the doors of the kingdom of light to operate through us. The same occurs when we operate in forgiveness, in righteousness, in compassion and in mercy. By allowing these good things into our lives, we are able to make an alliance with God's kingdom, which then allows the Holy Spirit to operate within us so he can guide us to reach the destiny that God has designed for each one of us.

Another good reason to practice loving one another and seeking God's righteousness is that it binds all evil works of the kingdom of darkness in our lives. When we are walking in the principles of God's kingdom and establish them as thefoundation for our lives, we are actively blocking any access of the spirit of injustice and leaving it with no authority over us. In fact, when we practice righteousness, we activate the very good cycles of justice and blessings over our lives. It's because we are operating under God's kingdom and his principles that we are able to release all the awesome weight that the kingdom of God carries.

Allow me to emphasize this: the best way to get rid of the spirit of injustice is to make sure we become true representatives of what the Lord has taught us through the perfect example of his Son, Jesus Christ, which is to *love one another*!

Whoever does not love, does not know God, because God is love. (1 John 4:8 NIV)

> Above all, love each other deeply, because love covers over a multitude of sins. (1 Pet. 4:8 NIV)

The reason we should love one another is that it's such a big blow to the spirit of injustice! When we love our neighbors, we don't want to trick them, we don't want to make false testimony against them, we don't want to abuse them, and we certainly don't want to kill them or enslave them. All we need to do is to treat them the same way we would want them to treat us. Now we know why God is so persistent in wanting us to love our neighbors as ourselves! The following arebiblical verses that reinforce everything we have discussed:

> These are the things you are to do: 'Speak the truth to each other, and render true and sound judgment in your courts; do not plot evil against your neighbor, and do not love to swear falsely. I hate all this,' declares The Lord. (Zech. 8:16-17 NIV)

> Keep on loving each other as brothers. (Heb. 13:1 NIV)

> Therefore, there is now no condemnation for those who are in Christ Jesus, because through Christ Jesus the law of the Spirit of life set me free from the law of sin and death. (Rom. 8:1-2 NIV)

> You are the light of the world. A city on a hill cannot be hidden. (Matt. 5:14 NIV)

You are the salt of the earth. But if the salt loses its saltiness, how can it be made salty again? (Matt. 5:13 NIV)

But seek first his kingdom and his righteousness, and all these things will be given to you as well. (Matt. 6:33 NIV)

Be devoted to one another in brotherly love. Honor one another above yourselves. (Rom. 12:10 NIV)

Jesus said, 'My kingdom is not of this world. If it were, my servants would fight to prevent my arrest by the Jews. But now my kingdom is from another place. (John 18:36 NIV)

Do not conform any longer to the pattern of this world, but be transformed by the renewing of your mind. (Rom. 12:2 NIV)

Follow my example, as I follow the example of Christ. (1 Cor. 11: 1 NIV)

In your anger do not sin. Do not let the sun go down while you are still angry, and do not give the devil a foothold. (Eph. 4:26 NIV)

For you were once darkness, but now you are light in the Lord. (Eph. 5:8 NIV)

These are the things we must follow in order to shut the doors of our lives, family and nation to the kingdom of darkness and its unjust government, and to start working on the great commission to establish God's kingdom andrighteousness on this earth. Our ultimate goal is to reach all nations with the knowledge of God's Word, so everyone can enjoy the atmosphere of love, peace, justice, compassion and a justice that comes from God's kingdom.

ANGELA STRONG.

BIBLIOGRAPHY

"Modern Slavery and Child Labour." International Labour Organization. Last modified September 19, 2017. https://www.ilo.org/global/about-the-ilo/newsroom/news/WCMS_574717/lang--en/index.htm.

"11 Facts About Human Trafficking." DoSomething.org. Accessed February 11, 2019. https://www.dosomething.org/us/facts/11-facts-about-human-trafficking.

[1] "Modern Slavery and Child Labour," International Labour Organization, last modified September 19, 2017. https://www.ilo.org/global/about-the-ilo/newsroom/news/WCMS_574717/lang--en/index.htm.

[2] "11 Facts About Human Trafficking," DoSomething.Org, accessed February 11, 2019. https://www.dosomething.org/us/facts/11-facts-about-human-trafficking

CPSIA information can be obtained
at www.ICGtesting.com
Printed in the USA
BVHW071152010419

544231BV00009B/194/P

9 781973 656937